T0312322

Cambridge Elements ≡

Elements in Music and the City
edited by
Simon McVeigh
University of London
Abigail Wood
University of Haifa

BACKGROUND MUSIC CULTURES IN FINNISH URBAN LIFE

Heikki Uimonen
University of Eastern Finland
Kaarina Kilpiö
Sibelius Academy, Uniarts Helsinki
Meri Kytö
University of Turku

CAMBRIDGE
UNIVERSITY PRESS

Shaftesbury Road, Cambridge CB2 8EA, United Kingdom

One Liberty Plaza, 20th Floor, New York, NY 10006, USA

477 Williamstown Road, Port Melbourne, VIC 3207, Australia

314–321, 3rd Floor, Plot 3, Splendor Forum, Jasola District Centre, New Delhi – 110025, India

103 Penang Road, #05–06/07, Visioncrest Commercial, Singapore 238467

Cambridge University Press is part of Cambridge University Press & Assessment, a department of the University of Cambridge.

We share the University's mission to contribute to society through the pursuit of education, learning and research at the highest international levels of excellence.

www.cambridge.org
Information on this title: www.cambridge.org/9781009486934

DOI: 10.1017/9781009374682

First published 2024

A catalogue record for this publication is available from the British Library.

ISBN 978-1-009-48693-4 Hardback
ISBN 978-1-009-37467-5 Paperback
ISSN 2633-3880 (online)
ISSN 2633-3872 (print)

Cambridge University Press & Assessment has no responsibility for the persistence or accuracy of URLs for external or third-party internet websites referred to in this publication and does not guarantee that any content on such websites is, or will remain, accurate or appropriate.

Background Music Cultures in Finnish Urban Life

Elements in Music and the City

DOI: 10.1017/9781009374682
First published online: April 2024

Heikki Uimonen
University of Eastern Finland

Kaarina Kilpiö
Sibelius Academy, Uniarts Helsinki

Meri Kytö
University of Turku

Author for correspondence: Heikki Uimonen, heikki.uimonen@uef.fi

Abstract: This Element focuses on how music is experienced, articulated, and reclaimed in urban commercial environments. Special attention is paid to listeners, spaces, and music, co- and re-produced continuously in their triangular relationship affected by social, legal, economic, and technological factors. The study of the historical development of background music industries, construction of contemporary sonic environments, and individual meaning-making is based on extensive data gathered through interviews, surveys, and fieldwork, and supported by archival research. Due to the Finnish context and the ethnomusicological approach, this study is culture-sensitive, providing a fresh 'factory-to-consumer' perspective on a phenomenon generally understood as industry-lead, behavioural, and global. This title is also available as Open Access on Cambridge Core.

Keywords: background music, anthropology of sound, muzak, sonic environment, urban space

ISBNs: 9781009486934 (HB), 9781009374675 (PB), 9781009374682 (OC)
ISSNs: 2633-3880 (online), 2633-3872 (print)

Contents

1 Introduction

'Do you get more done when music is playing?'[1]

In 1970, the City of Helsinki decided to conduct an experiment at three of its premises aimed at studying the effects of using Muzak products. The experiment focused on employee satisfaction, self-perceived work performance, measured productivity, and customer impressions. The endeavour was inspired by a proposition from Finnestrad, the local Muzak franchisee. A project report (City of Helsinki 1970) was archived in the personal files of Mr Eero Vallila, the owner and chief executive of the company, and found decades later by background music researchers.

The music system was installed on the shop floor where employees worked in the city's central laundry department and the car repair shop of their building office. For assessment in customer service premises, the city chose its child welfare office. A survey was conducted charting the views of the employees and measuring the efficiency of their work. Interestingly, the question the survey asked regarding choosing an option other than Muzak offered only one alternative, the Finnish public radio music programme Sävelradio (see subsection 4.2).

From the point of view of Finnestrad, the results were disappointing. Contentedness was deemed 'fairly good' in the employee sample and 'good' in the child welfare customer sample. No increase in either efficiency or productivity was detected. The outcome was precisely opposite to the marketing message Muzak was attempting to convince potential clients of at the time: that any music could entertain people, but it took scientifically tested Muzak to make organisations and businesses churn out more profit and productivity. In the end, the report did not recommend making Muzak a part of the city employees' workdays; it did, however, recommend that a subscription to the Muzak system be procured for the customer service space of the child welfare offices.[2]

This episode touches on at least three points relevant to this Element. Firstly, the power of music – however ingeniously tailored – to bring about intended results is and always has been limited and subject to a multitude of variables. Secondly, the historical changes in music cultures have significantly affected the market trends for functional music products: the idea of entertaining child welfare customers with background music products using taxpayer money would probably sound alien in any decade other than the 1960s and 1970s.

---

[1] City of Helsinki (1970), Appendix 3: question sheet.
[2] Documentation about acquiring the system for the child welfare premises has not survived but, in 1971, the city seems to have installed a Muzak system in at least one healthcare unit. Vallila made several subsequent attempts to get a contract with the city, including donating music systems to city administrative units for limited periods.

Thirdly, the prevailing music culture of the time invariably affects the discussion and circumstances surrounding background music: employees given one alternative to Muzak – Sävelradio – might reveal a preference for it in their responses, which they did. The result, however, says more about the music listening culture in Finland in 1970 than any universal boost in work capacity, atmosphere, or general productivity as a result of either alternative.

Background Music Cultures in Finnish Urban Life is inspired by these kinds of observations of the past and present cultural conditions of using functional music in everyday life. It is the first concise ethnomusicological, sensory ethnography-oriented, and fieldwork-based analysis of music in urban environments, drawing from our research project ACMESOCS: Auditory Cultures, Mediated Sounds and Constructed Spaces (2019–22). This Academy of Finland funded research takes auditory culture and the materiality of background music practices seriously and analyses them as part of sonic environments and their socio-spatial contingencies.[3] The project's three research strands scrutinised (1) the development of the commercial sonic environment and its implied human object, the listener-consumer, referring to the target group of the background music industry – at whom its message has been and is currently aimed; (2) economic, technological, legislative, organisational, and cultural factors transforming urban acoustic environments in the context of ubiquitous music, including novel products like the generative software used in creating branded musical ambience; and (3) experienced and reclaimed acoustic environments to understand people's experiences, perceptions, and actions in urban and commercial environments, especially regarding ubiquitous musics.

Researching urban auditory cultures, ACMESOCS focused on how these are experienced, articulated, and reclaimed. We are interested in shedding light on social, legal, economic, and technological factors that have an effect on the historical development of the background and foreground of the music industry, on the construction of contemporary sonic environments, and on the use of individual meaning-making in various public and commercial environments. The aim is to include a diversity of listening and experiencing and to give room to a range of approaches by introducing the added precision of crowdsourced and field materials.[4]

Although the relationship between music, place, and listening has been extensively studied (see e.g. Stockfelt 1994; Born 2013; Section 2 in this Element), interest in background music specifically has been somewhat limited.

[3] This publication is funded by the Academy of Finland.
[4] The ACMESOCS field materials are referred to as follows: ACMEf = fieldwork notes; ACMEi = interviews; ACMEp = photos; ACMEs = surveys conducted by the project.

This Element analyses a combination of the agency of the groups that are designing and experiencing background music: producers, people working in environments filled with background music, and city dwellers, who are often cast in the role of consumers. This approach sheds light on the functionality of background music beyond more general notions of sales promotion and customer persuasion. Background music has also frequently been portrayed in research as a uniform phenomenon, or even as an identifiable musical genre. In our view, the state of play is rather a plurality of background music cultures: certain shared global marketing logics and functions with considerable differences in local emphasis.

Compared to the often sleek and smooth design of playlists, the experience of music among the urban din is often more rudimentary. Urban dwellers participate in and pass through living acoustic environments where they encounter lo-fi technology in playback systems: muffled and compressed music, barely audible between layers of hums, voices, and sounds. The most common situation in which one encounters background music is moving past loudspeakers in hallways and stores. This causes the music to be heard in dynamic glides, waves of intensifying and weakening sounds, momentary and random, presenting us with methodological questions: which parts of the 'music not being listened to' are actually audible to start with, and to whom – how is it relevant, and how can this relevance be studied? How can the diversity of the listeners and their listening abilities be considered as a relevant aspect with regard to the urban experience of music?

We explore background music as a central dimension of modern and postmodern urbanity. Music has a long history as a part of commerce, marketing, and consumption, as well as a fundamental part of urban culture. We propose that background music as a phenomenon is, by definition, tied to the figure of the *listener-consumer*, the modern urbanite who is, on one hand, a creation of the advertising industry and, on the other, an individual within a mediatised music culture who is able to *dishearken* (*borthöra*, Stockfelt 1994: 20), or pay no attention to music. Referencing the formulations of mediated urbanity and urban media studies (Tosoni & Ridell 2016), where urban space is seen as a networked and bodily context of media consumption, this Element brings forth the densely mediated and overlapping acoustic realities that are embedded in the urban fabric, woven into the very infrastructure and material conditions of urban space. Background music makes urban spaces recognisable, negotiable, and distinctive. Playing background music is a mediatised place-making process through which urbanity can be listened to.

Our point of departure is to study background music as culture. Studying music as culture may identify how societal values such as hierarchy or individualism are reflected in musical conceptualisation, behaviour, and sound (Nettl 1983/2005: 217–18). Researching music as humanly organised sound in given circumstances refers to not only the end product but also process and activity. This includes the interactions between human beings, motivations behind their behaviours, and the significance they attach to them. These intellectual, physical, cultural, and social dynamics and processes generate musical products. Music is made perceptually, conceptually, and emotionally. This process, termed as *musicking*, refers to how music is not just made but also responded and assigned meaning to. (See Blacking 1973; Small 1998; Rice 2014: 5–6, 9.)

Tia DeNora's seminal *Music in Everyday Life* (2000), based on fieldwork carried out in the 1990s, provided a wide-ranging account of people and music in everyday life in Britain. In our Finnish research setting, we focus on one phenomenon within everyday musical experience: the use of background music. We go further in contextualising it in its 'unsolicited' form, holding on to the experiential approach while also including the structures of the contemporary digital background of the music industry and its spatial and cultural manifestations. As an enhancement of a culture-specific analysis of the Finnish case, this Element provides a methodological tool applicable to understanding 'background music in culture X'. This model will enable taking into account specific features of each local culture – for example, those related to music, sound, the service sector, urban architecture, public and commercial broadcasting, and the mediascape as a whole.

Contrary to popular media discourse that treats background music as one-dimensional or manipulative, this Element offers a broader understanding of music culture as an historical and spatiotemporally bound phenomenon for the non-expert in the field. Based on extensive ethnographic data gathered through interviews, surveys, and fieldwork (such as listening walks and participatory observation), and supported by archival research, it will also present a novel data-gathering method, suitable for collecting information on everyday experiential phenomena as ephemeral as background music. This approach, combining walking methods, mapping, sound diaries, crowdsourcing, and use of music recognition apps and instant messaging, can be applied to educational projects, for example. We tap into examples like the use of music during the Christmas season, in shopping malls or sex shops, and historical cases like background music in primary schools, and so on. The sections delve into the profession of the background music designer/producer as well as the working environment of the cashier and the restaurant patron, among others. Finland, with its particularities in urban and environmental structures, along with its economic and music industry history, is our research context. Despite its cultural focus, the methodology and theoretical considerations in this Element are applicable to other countries and contexts.

An essential part of the cultural study of background music is the examination of the materiality of sound – aspects such as the spaces and systems that reproduce sound and how they function. Technology plays an essential role in the quality of the sound of music and how that sound carries to different parts of a given space. Among the factors influencing the outcome are the type of loudspeaker system and its age, how the system is built, the number of speakers, and the extent of the infrastructure on which the system depends for its functionality (Wi-Fi, power grid, system design, installation, maintenance, and repair). Integrated sound systems with dozens of loudspeakers can be almost invisible and thus accentuate the idea of the control of the system as being remote and disconnected.

This Element helps in building the reader's awareness and skills that create 'functional music literacy' (cf. 'media literacy'). This means an understanding of, for example, the agencies, spatial factors, and cultural conventions at play in urban commercial spaces with music. Background music processes are viewed as music cultures, taking form from ideologies, institutions, infrastructures, and material objects. The background music industry caters to culturally diverse ears, and the circumstances in which it is consumed vary likewise. Due to the Finnish context and the ethnomusicological approach, the study is culture-sensitive and specific, providing a fresh perspective on a phenomenon generally understood as industry-led, behavioural, and global.

The structure of this Element follows the lines of background music production – 'from the factory to the consumer', so to speak. In this section, we map out the concept of background music along its contingencies and present some relevant scholarly discussion from recent years. A contextualising section follows, explaining how we understand the Finnish context of the study and how different cultural, societal, and infrastructural characteristics shape the culture of background music locally. This section demonstrates the historical formation (from the 1960s until today) of the *listener-consumer*, that is, the model audience member for sonic advertising, and also deals with the early years of the background music industry in Finland. In the third section, based on extensive interviews, we elaborate how companies providing background music services operate and how they see themselves as actors in the fields of music and advertising. Publicly funded and commercial radio stations will also be presented as providers of background music. The following section moves from the production of background music services to the commercial space and to the service sector, consisting of people listening to background music several hours a day. This section, based on a large survey, interviews, and fieldwork observations, examines how people work with 'music not chosen' and how they understand it as affecting their well-being. The fifth section focuses on the so-called end users of background music, the urban dwellers, and their everyday encounters with it. A case analysis demonstrating a seasonal disruption (Christmas) in the everyday implementation of background music aims to develop a toolkit of ethnographic methods suitable for a dense urban environment. In the last section, we discuss some current changes in the field and present a methodological checklist for studying background music that we hope will inspire students and researchers interested in the urban, music, and auditory culture.

2 Mapping Background Music as a Phenomenon

Background music as a phenomenon is multifaceted, and there are various perspectives from which to view it. Working towards a definition for this research, we start from the following: by *background music*, we mean mediated music played non-stop in commercial and public spaces, supporting/ assisting/accompanying other activities of a target group/city dwellers, with a function related to commercial profitability or work productivity. It is also usually created for temporary enjoyment and selected by someone (at the 'factory') not expecting the listener (the 'consumer') to stay and focus on the music.

To elaborate further on this historically and locally changing use of music, some analytical questions focusing on its infrastructural, social, economic, and ideological aspects can be helpful. The entanglement of these diverse topics is outlined in what follows (see Figure 1).

Though not to be read as too hierarchical or definitive but rather as dismantling the phenomenon of background music to gain analytical insight, Figure 1 specifies seven approaches in the form of questions: Where is it played? What is the playback medium? Who is the music collated by? Who regulates it? For whom is it played and how is it perceived? And, finally, for what ends is it played? The questions mentioned here are related to the concept of agency in background music, which is crucial in any study of music or sound in an ethnomusicological or anthropological context. In this study, the concept of agency refers to individual and collective capacities for action in music-related settings (Karlsen 2019; Section 5). The diverse agencies are manifested sonically in specific contexts of time, place, and listener.

The city, a dense geographic concentration of people and things, can be understood as a form of music as well. The density of the soundscape (perceived as the increasing number of loudspeakers) has stirred up a critique of 'piped music', a discussion similar to the environmental concern of urban habitats in the 1960s: mechanised music and PA systems were discussed as a form of pollution and excess detrimental to a healthy environment. This discourse on

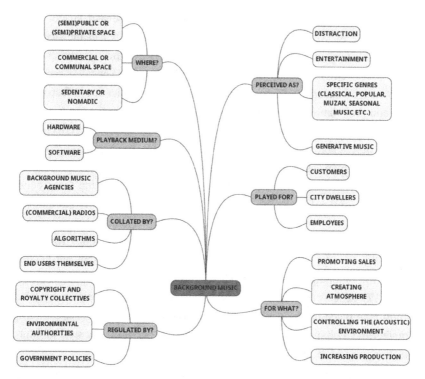

Figure 1 Contextual vivisection of the phenomenon of background music. Left: the nature of built space and the technology used for playback can be seen as infrastructural elements. Bottom left-hand corner: we understand collating and regulating as agency-related categories. Right: the perception of background music can be analysed on the level of experience. Bottom right-hand corner: categories related to the function and targeting of played music.

noise pollution is still very much present in discussions about the use of city space and urban community life. The uninterrupted sonic presence of background music is characteristic of media technologies that help in urban spatial organisation and navigation. Our 'factory-to-consumer' point of departure resonates with urban studies in its interest in the planning and designing of space and how it is re-made through practical use, incorporating communication technologies as necessary equipment (see Krajina & Stevenson 2020: 2).

Background music – like work uniforms – is a material practice that has emerged with modernity in the service industries. Whereas uniforms are more generally the result of an 'extreme rationalisation of appearance' (Tynan & Godson 2019: 2, 4), background music can be characterised as a sonic and spatial manifestation of a similar rational approach. Both are related to a fundamental transformation of the experience of time and space in the everyday life of Western capitalist societies in the first half of the twentieth century. The work uniform enables clients to identify members of staff and also marks service employees as working in and belonging to the business premises. In the case of background music, the identifying and orienting effect is less clear, and the relationship of both the workers and the customers to the sound material can be ambiguous, sometimes subject to negotiation and reflection.

The different notions of background music itself are somewhat contradictory. Anahid Kassabian states that there is no commonly agreed name for music not chosen by the listener. 'Background music' is sometimes in the foreground; 'business music' refers to the economic role of the music; 'environmental music' refers to its role in forming contexts; and 'programmed music' refers to its production and distribution, leaving out its consumption. Kassabian prefers the concept of 'ubiquitous musics' being always present but beyond our control, 'slipping under our thresholds of consciousness' (Kassabian 1999/2006: 117). Affects such as bodily responses to background music or any other stimuli take place before conscious understanding. These responses pass into thoughts and feelings, leaving behind a residue that becomes 'the stuff of future affective responses' (Kassabian 2013: xiii–xv).

The term 'ubiquitous music' covers multiple listening experiences, starting from radio, which has historically provided a wide range of musics for ubiquitous listening. With the advent of digital listening technologies, people have unprecedented control over what they listen to in their everyday life. There is no link between specific listening approaches and specific music styles, nor can ubiquitous or background music be identified as a particular genre. 'Shopping, sleeping, and secretarial work take place in such radically different contexts and across such radically diverse demographic or identity groups that there is no reasonable way of labeling ubiquitous musics and genre in any ways in which the term is generally used' (Boschi et al. 2013: 6–7). Instead of a specific style of music, we need to concentrate on the *alleged function* of music, since almost any music genre can be selected for use as ubiquitous or background music. Apart from listening, we also study other ways of interacting with music, such as dancing and singing.

Ubiquitous musics can be defined by their relationships to listening and attention and by their description as 'musical events that take place alongside other activities' (Boschi et al. 2013: 6–7). The significance of the act of listening stands out, for example in the background music companies' attempts at catering to diverse ears. In 1981, a former Muzak representative in Finland wrote in an opinion piece that, unlike the content he described as 'distracting' background music, their content was 'not meant to be listened to but heard' (*Helsingin Sanomat* 1981). As an illustrative example of the shift in background music culture, many current businesses in the trade have a reverse marketing strategy: instead of inquiring about their clients' own preferences for and conceptions of music, companies provide them with diverse music compilations, encouraging them to base their procurement decisions on listening.

In spite of undeniable similarities with ubiquitous music, we decided to use the concept of background music in this Element. *Ubiquitous music* and *ubiquitous listening* were coined for scholarly use – as tools for academic work. Background music is a concept used in the communication between representatives of the background music industry and their customers, as well as in the media, when music used in public spaces is commented on and discussed. This is also the concept we used while interacting with the participants of our research.

Conceptually, this Element draws from *soundscapes* and *sonic environments*, often used synonymously (Schafer 1977: 274), although soundscapes emphasise how individuals and society understand an acoustic environment through listening (Truax 2001: xviii). In given contexts, background music can be characterised as a form of a sonic environment, referring to sound's immersive qualities since the word 'environ' connotes 'surrounding' and 'enclosing'. Our auditory field encompasses 360 degrees, whereas the concept of *soundscape* has visual connotations, thus referring to panoramic perception (Uimonen 2020b: 58). Drawing from Pinch and Bijsterveld (2004) and Kassabian (2013), the concept of a 'sound environment' was coined to describe a relationship between music, audiences, and everyday life. It includes variables such as space, time, body, and choice of the technology needed for the diffusion and consumption of music. This approach not only should include issues such as gender, race, and ethnicity (Nowak & Bennett 2014: 442) but also should be refined to take culture-specific, historical, or language-related aspects of music consumption into consideration – especially in the context of background music.

In this Element, we do not aim to propose an overarching concept in understanding background music and its diverse contexts. Its strength lies in understanding how the whole *from-the-factory-to-the-consumer* chain operates in everyday life – a concept often used in vague articulations of musical significance in different contexts and spaces (Nowak & Bennett 2014). Music and the everyday are connected to time, and therefore to routines and repetitions: 'events that happen every night or every week, even every month and every year are part of mundane, ordinary living' (Hesmondhalgh 2002: 125–6). In this respect, background music can be viewed as one subcategory of *staple music* (Uimonen 2014). In the latter half of the twentieth century, sound-reproducing technologies became widely available and commonplace and, more importantly, part of everyday practices. Unlike gramophone records, which could only be purchased from specialised shops, compact cassettes were available from Finnish grocery stores, supermarkets, and service stations, like other staple products, from the 1970s. Music consumption changed because of music's availability and new dissemination channels. (Kilpiö et al. 2015: 31.)

Commenting on the history of recorded music and its social effects in *Performing Rites* (1998: 236), Simon Frith concluded music was everywhere and no longer in need of framing via a special place or time: 'there is less and less sense of music being "appropriate" to certain times and places'. Recording and transmission enabled new uses of music, especially when used to accompany everyday life at work and during leisure time in diverse environments – a phenomenon characterised as 'transphonia' (Uimonen 2005). Technologically mediated listening situations demanded new or 'adequate' modes of listening: the 'situation in which one encounters music conditions music itself', and a listener needs competence not only to listen but also to dishearken music (Stockfelt 1994: 20; 1997) – or not to interact with music in any other sensorial way. Music has also become mobile and follows its users practically everywhere (Frith 1998: 236; see also Tagg 1984). Frith's comment on music and place holds true thirty years later, with augmented dimensions. With ubiquitous mobile phone networks and Wi-Fi connections, users of digital services are online continuously, even when asleep. This lays the foundation for contemporary 24/7 uses of music.

Contemporary staple music is a phenomenon with lots of potential scholarly interest. It is undoubtedly connected to urbanism but not inherently urban in itself: rather, with staple music, urbanity can be brought into almost any environment. Its uses are diverse, and they have manifested in birdsong in public lavatories (like in the Helsinki-Vantaa airport), music used in museums and installations – or, recently, a Spotify playlist compiled by the Finnish state-owned railway company, advertised on cardboard coffee cups used in the trains' restaurant cars and accessible through a QR-code and the passengers' own mobile devices as a 'gift' from the train company.

3 Scholarly Approaches to Background Music

As a modern and ubiquitous phenomenon, background music has been approached by different academic disciplines with different research interests. These have included psychology of music, historical research, sociology of music, musicology, ethnomusicology, and sound studies. Case studies have scrutinised topics such as music and violence (Johnson & Cloonan 2009), the relationship of music, youths, and everyday life (Nowak & Bennett 2014), annoying music (Trotta 2020), the philosophy of ambient sound (Schmidt 2023), the influence of background music in wine selection (North et al. 1999), and whether romantic music influences consumer behaviour in a florist shop (Jacob et al. 2009).

There is an extensive body of research on how stores use music to evoke reactions in customers and, further, to influence customers' decision-making. This has been studied, for example, from the viewpoint of premises playing loud music to increase activity or fast music to pace the in-door traffic flow (Smith & Curnow 1966; Milliman 1982), and the interactive effect on music tempo and mode (minor key) on in-door sales (Knöferle et al. 2011). It has also been suggested that music modifies people's first impressions of products (Zander 2006) and influences their choices when deciding between two competing foods (Yeoh & North 2010); and that background and foreground music shapes emotional responses in the mall (Kang & Yi 2019 – carried out in a laboratory setting). The majority of these studies represent disciplines differing from a culturally sensitive research paradigm and are interested in consumer behaviour rather than diverse agencies changing, experiencing, and affecting background music.

Commercial environments are being built with a thorough understanding as well as exploitation of the use of several stimuli simultaneously, such as lights, scents, visuals, and sound, to create desired atmospheres and to influence the consumer's purchasing intentions (Spence et al. 2014). The formal and practical knowledge of responses and a wide range of new technologies have led to a situation in which affective responses 'can be designed into spaces, often out of what seems like very little at all' (Thrift 2004: 67–8). At a Starbucks coffee shop, this can mean 'everything from the obvious, like sofas and fabrics and wood and color schemes, to the subtle, like how few CDs to have available or font choices for signs, is carefully selected to create a particular affective response' (Kassabian 2013: 91).

Contemporary circumstances of experiencing background music are thus somewhat different from the musicking settings that had been of academic interest until the 1980s. New questions and approaches became necessary. As one of the first scholars to take an interest in the area, and specifically Muzak, Ronald Radano considered the shift in aesthetic experience produced by what he called 'consensus music', urging for a new approach recognising 'both levels of musical awareness, one reflective and the other nonreflective' (Radano 1989: 458). Especially in urban spaces designed for consumption, background music is usually omnipresent, sometimes also overlapping with other music and sound sources: several pieces of music can be heard in a given place at the same time.

Emily Thompson explains in *The Soundscape of Modernity: Architectural Acoustics and the Culture of Listening in America 1900–1933* how scientists and engineers manipulated material and architectural constructions to control sound in urban space. The environments converted can be characterised as modern. Firstly, they were efficient and stripped down of sounds considered unnecessary. Secondly, they advanced efficient behaviour in those who heard or listened to them by minimising noise and maximising productivity. Thirdly, they were also modern by becoming products and commodities in a culture defined by the act of consumption and evaluated by the listeners. Moreover, 'man's technical mastery over his physical environment' and nature transformed traditional relationships between sound, space, and time. (Thompson 2002: 2–4.) Although Thompson's book deals predominantly with architectural acoustics, the phenomena observed also set the stage for the use of background music. Furthermore, technologically mediated musical sounds and reorganised sonic environments resulted in emerging new trends of listening.

Pre-industrialisation manual work was often accompanied by singing to coordinate and pace work and to provide aesthetic pleasure and stimulation. Music was related directly to work through its rhythms, the sounds of the tools, and physical movement. Mechanisation and regulation of work during the industrial period diminished this need and function, and noisy machines made singing impractical. During the Fordist industrialisation in the twentieth century, broadcast music was introduced in British and US workplaces from the top down, following the theories by Frederick Taylor and aimed at controlling the labour process. In contemporary contexts, with professionals engaged in mental work, music is often listened to individually by workers or broadcast in service settings. (Dibben & Haake 2013: 151–2.)

Pre- and post-industrial uses of music can be characterised as two separate phases or ages using unmediated and mediated music, respectively. Unmediated music refers predominantly to acoustically transmitted, oral, and thus unique music, whereas mediated music means widely available, printed, recorded, and electronically and digitally mediated music (Kurkela et al. 2009: 3). Sensed environments are not only interpreted but actively produced within the triangular relationship among the sensing individual, the environment, and sensorial information, as suggested by Steven Feld (1996: 91): 'As place is sensed, senses are placed; as places make sense, senses make place.' The notion resonates with Georgina Born's ideas of music, sound, and space intertwining in complex ways. Music and sounds are mediated by subjectivity, corporeity, and movement through location. In addition, social multiplicity of the same space of subjects constitutes new social relations. Also, temporal mediation transforms the constellation of sound and space in a given acoustic environment. (Born 2013: 19.) Lived experience involves constant shifts in sensory figures and potentials for multisensory interactions.

Like any other music, background music can be interpreted as constructing self-identity – 'as a device for reflexive process of remembering/constructing who one is' (DeNora 2000: 63). It may not be selected by the person who happens to hear it, but it still affords an opportunity for active listening and memory retrieval. Ethnomusicology and anthropology of sound both approach music and sounds as human culture, looking past music's stimulus or influence on its listeners, or the assumption that listeners could be reduced to simply passive receivers of music. This approach is in line with contemporary ideas of the power of music as constructed by the listener interacting with the music.

Scholarly interests have also reflected the changes in the background music industry and their manifestations in urban space, as well as reactions to mediated music in public places. In their promotion of acoustic design and improvement of sonic environments, early soundscape scholars and pedagogists took a critical stance towards background music and considered it inherently dubious. Part of this can be explained by Muzak Corporation's widespread presence in the 1960s and 1970s, criticised by soundscape scholars oriented towards Western classical music and related listening practices. The time was ripe for criticism: in 1969, the General Assembly of the International Music Council of UNESCO passed a resolution on 'abusive use, in private and public places, of recorded or broadcast music' (see Schafer 1977: 97–8).

Composer and pedagogue R. Murray Schafer rightly concluded that 'for the first time in history an international organisation involved primarily with the *production* of sounds suddenly turned its attention to their *reduction*' (Schafer 1977: 97–8; italics in original). The statement aimed at reducing music was motivated by surprising and in some cases unwanted encounters with background music, indicating an increase of its use. Violinist Yehudi Menuhin, who served on the Council's Executive Committee, rebelled against having to be a 'captive audience' in an airplane playing background music (Lanza 1995: 153). Background music was equally disliked by the younger generation of popular music listeners. When the rock and folk music of the 1960s began to tackle issues related to culture, politics, and sexuality, the easy-listening arrangements of 'Muzak's bowdlerized hits seemed more and more like an affront' (New Yorker 2006). Already in the late 1960s, a small company called Yesco challenged Muzak by selling what it called foreground music (Baumgarten 2012). This change of business logic – replacing background music with foreground music – is described by Jonathan Sterne as follows: 'Why listen to cheesy remakes when you can hear the original?' Muzak jumped on the foreground bandwagon in 1983 (Sterne 2013: 124) and launched its Foreground Music One channel in 1985. Foreground music's momentum coincided with lifestyle research trends in their attempt to study particularly 'the post-hippie hyper-individuals' and their preferences, including music (Lanza 2013: 623).

Michael Bull (2013: 630–1) analyses sonic mediation through the filter of technologies that afford responses among city dwellers as *Fordist, post-Fordist* and *hyper-post-Fordist*. The first one refers to collectively experienced technologies colonising social spaces, for example shopping centres; post-Fordist refers to niche marketing, for example music played in specific shops to provide the correct ambience for shopping; and hyper-post-Fordist refers to mobile technologies and their users creating individualised soundscapes for themselves. It is essential to understand that all three sound experiences exist simultaneously.

In his 1997 article on music in shopping centres, Jonathan Sterne finds similarities between foreground music and radio content and clarifies the programming logic called quantum modulation. Unlike background music's attempt at gradual mood changes, foreground music aims for an unchanging mood. Quantum modulation maintains flow with the help of numerical values based on diverse criteria such as rhythm, tempo, artist, and genre. With the use of cross-fading, the transitions from song to song are seamless. It is assumed that listeners will hear music for a short duration, for example when visiting a shop (Sterne 1997: 32). In essence, quantum modulation appears to be an elaborately named trademark developed by Muzak for categorising and selecting foreground music for different purposes as well as making their content stand out from parity products by competitors.

Sterne (2013: 123) calls programmed music services a 'second-order media economy': they utilise music already circulated as a commodity and familiar to listeners. 'Programmed music requires an earlier, "first" moment of circulation, prior to its own'. Second-order economy programmed music has also challenged scholars to rethink schemes of 'production' and 'consumption'. This applies not only to programmed music: the same principles of second-media economy hold true with radio foreground music playlists, compiled of familiar songs and tunes targeted to given audiences for everyday listening in different environments.

Finnish scholarly literature emphasises the culture-specific nature of background music. Despite being a part of the transnational music industry, background music practices in Finland are framed by conditions such as language issues or national legislation. Contributions include publications from ethnomusicologists, social historians, and soundscape researchers, with interests in practices transforming sonic environments. These include Muzak, use of radio in the workplace, and on-hold music, as well as music at department stores and shopping malls. (See e.g. Kilpiö 2005 & 2011; Ranta 2005; Kokko 2016; Kontukoski & Uimonen 2019.)

Background music providers and their clients want listeners and consumers to feel a certain way in stores or in other premises. The transnational challenge they face is that they 'can no more guarantee listener's responses to the music than the producer of any cultural text can guarantee its meaning in advance' (Sterne 2013: 126). As a result, they rely on existing recordings while aiming to increase production or consumption. Programmed music's ability to elicit responses in listeners is constantly underlined in both background music promoters' behavioural psychological explanations and ideological criticisms of (mis)use of music. However, like any other product 'its purchasers buy it on its promise' (Sterne 2013: 126). Music does not act upon an individual as a stimulus. Its effect is the result of how individuals orient to it and how they interpret it, not to mention how they 'place it within their personal musical maps' of extra-musical associations (DeNora 2000: 61). Although not commonly admitted among background music entrepreneurs, this is precisely what the CEO of one of the major companies pointed out to us in an interview quite straightforwardly. When asked if research of music was a matter of importance in their line of business, he stated how customer behaviour is affected by 'current weather' or issues such as 'what Trump just said and what is going on in the South China Sea . . . whatever happens in an individual's environment will have a strong effect on his/her consumer behaviour. It is difficult to say whether it was this specific music that we played that caused the collapse or increase of sales'. (ACMEi 2020c.)

What has remained largely unanswered and marginal in research is culture-sensitive contextualisation. Background music has often been viewed as a generic, global phenomenon, depleted of cultural characteristics. The conception has never been fully comprehensive, and accuracy has crumbled with each decade and development towards the end of the twentieth century. Specific culture-historical environments restrict, enable, and frame matters such as language used in song lyrics, national and regional transformation of technological environments, and possible differences and similarities in background music selection practices. This holds true especially in non-English-speaking countries (not to say that specific and diverse background music cultures would not exist in English-speaking cultures). Since this Element has taken the question of cultural dependence as one of the themes we wish to explore, we will next present the central socio-historical and cultural developments that form the backdrop to distinctive features in background music cultures in Finland. We hope to present, by first concentrating on a case of a small northern European country, an itemisation and a set of questions that will help with producing a framework for creating workable methods in various background music cultures.

4 Historical Context: Cultural, Societal, and Infrastructural Characteristics

In this section, we present a concise overview of the circumstances and developments in Finland, for the reader to better grasp the locally conditioned background music cultures. The country went through exceptionally rapid structural changes during the 1950s and 1960s. Urbanisation picked up steam: in 1950, the majority of the population lived in rural areas, but by the early 1980s, the tables had turned, and some 60 per cent of Finns resided in urban areas (in Germany, for instance, the same percentage had been registered in the 1910s).

One of the most dramatic changes took place in the balance within the Finnish economic structure. The primary sector shrunk to a fraction of its share of employees, while the service sector expanded swiftly from a minor sector of employment into the most important one from the beginning of the 1960s (Haapala & Peltola 2018: 205–6). The Finnish service culture, on the other hand, has been relatively slow in evolving from matter-of-fact conduct of affairs towards hospitality and 'giving people more than they expect', sometimes referred to in Finnish colloquial language as 'continental service culture'.

Private consumption also soared. The Finnish consumer society advanced considerably thanks to several developments: the edging away of post-war rationing, favourable circumstances in the world economy, structural changes in the local economy, and migration of the population to the cities (Valkonen 1985: 211). In the early 1960s, living standards in Finland began to rise rapidly, and people had more money at their disposal. The supply of consumer goods expanded considerably. Paid annual leave increased from 9–12 days to 18–24 days, enabling more spending on leisure and culture. Promises of progress and well-being were associated with an 'American lifestyle' and consumer culture, with central local players in trade and industry constantly reporting about their study trips to the United States. (Heinonen & Pantzar 2002: 44.) Background music systems were among the strategic solutions embraced widely in businesses with the aim of fulfilling these promises and 'boarding the train of progress'. The ideological and structural forces behind background music adoption are thus particularly distinguishable in Finland.

Face-to-face vocal advertising on the streets, markets, and village roads had faded in the early twentieth century. The Finnish urban soundscape was becoming more noise-laden, and forms of commerce were changing. Itinerant traders and service providers who advertised by shouting and singing in urban spaces gave way to electronically transmitted audio-visual advertising (Kilpiö 2001: 72–73), which gradually took off. An important aspect of consumerism for both the Finnish soundscape and city structure was motorisation, which happened 'late and swiftly' in Finland compared to the other Nordic countries (Bergholm 2001: 79–80). Between 1960 and 1973, the number of cars on Finnish roads and streets increased from around 255,000 to over 1 million, and continued to rise rapidly: by 1990, some 2.2 million cars had been registered for road use (ICRT 2022). The trend continued and strengthened, up to the point where Finland has become significantly more motorised than the rest of the Nordic countries (Ramsey 2022). From the point of view of soundscapes inherent to everyday life, this meant at least two developments: noise levels rose in street spaces, and hypermarkets became serious contenders for shopping and running errands in city centres. The insulated interiors of Finnish cars remained out of the advertisers' reach in Finland for several decades, however, since car radios only played the public broadcasting channels until the deregulation – or more precisely, re-regulation – of radio broadcasting in 1985. On the whole, the 1970s saw major changes in the Finns' outlooks on life. Emphasis on individuality and the pursuit of personal pleasure increased.

In restaurant premises, performing live music and playing recordings were closely supervised in Finland, mainly due to the strong position of local copyright organisations (Mäkelä 2017). For most Finns, dining out was not common before the 1980s. The educated upper classes had warned people against restaurants in the late nineteenth century as 'places where alcohol was served'. For decades, dining out was an elite custom, while many Finns kept shunning restaurants, on one hand assuming drunken depravity was going on inside, and on the other fearing they themselves would not master the intricate etiquette of restaurant culture. Finns who came of age in and after the 1980s showed a much more positive attitude towards dining and drinking out than the previous generations, and the range of different restaurants widened in Finnish cities. The somewhat negative image of Finnish restaurants also contributed to the 1960s and 1970s popularity of foreign concepts such as pizzerias, pubs, and Chinese restaurants. (Sillanpää 2002: 215.)

In terms of sonic environment, and background music in particular, frequenting so-called ethnic restaurants is an interesting development. Before the arrival of restaurant chains, individual restaurant owners usually played whatever music they thought culturally suitable and accurate atmosphere-wise, meaning that patrons of 'ethnic' restaurants possibly heard quite diverse sounds and rhythms. The precise musical content could be subject to negotiations, as a former sales representative recalls:

> We got records directly from somewhere in Italy ... Italian music; put together a compilation of it, and sent it on its way [to the customer] ... and

got lambasted. It wasn't supposed to be Italian music – it was supposed to be
Italo-pop, which isn't really typical Italian music at all, but Euro-pop from
Italy. (Hietanoro 2006)

Selecting songs was a time-consuming process, since one four-hour tape
required one hundred songs to be hand-picked (Hietanoro 2006). In the
1980s, the use of office and workplace music decreased, while the use of
music in restaurants and the retail sector increased (Paukku 2006). The supply
of background music evolved in line with changes in the Finnish restaurant
culture. The earlier division into bars, dance restaurants, and food restaurants
was challenged, and the restaurant chains and pizzerias introduced in the 1980s
democratised eating out into a family event.

Today, the Finnish retail sector is exceptionally concentrated – a state of
affairs recognised as a problem by the European Commission Directorate-
General for Competition (Hukari 2021: 13). Many reasons have been put
forward to explain the situation. Among these are the cold climate, forcing
consumers to limit their shopping to as few stores as possible; the passion for
cars among Finns, sustaining the hypermarkets and driving urban design
towards favouring and investing in them; the penny-pinching nature of the
Finnish people, driving people to cheaper and larger stores; and the tradition
of Finnish women as naturally belonging in the workforce and thus having
limited time available for daily shopping. Chiefly, however, the concentration
trend for the Finnish grocery trade was dictated by a strong takeover of
cooperative groups already in the 1930s. By the end of the 1960s, the plight
of small shops had accelerated: groups already accounted for 75 per cent of the
grocery market, and over the next ten years, the share rose to over 90 per cent.
(Komulainen 2018: 9–10: 237.)

The consequences for background music use are not clear-cut, partly since
our background music company interviewees did not comment on the effects of
the duopoly on contracts. Cooperative retail companies are managed regionally,
and unlike visual uniformity, the background music solutions seem to vary
slightly between regions. Unlike the cooperatives' visual appearance, their
background music is not uniform but is instead individually ordered from
different music providers by regional cooperatives (ACMEi 2022a). At the
individual level, some employees reflected on the state of play in our field
material: 'We think someone's making a load of money by selling [our
employer] that copyright-free music that's ever so horrible and features the
same pieces month after month'. (ACMEs/PAM 2021a.)

The cooperative retailing conglomerates had a significant role in expanding
the size of individual retailing units in the country as well. Several cooperative

groups made a purposeful effort in the 1960s to plan and promote a transformation in how daily consumer goods would be acquired in Finland (Hankonen 1994: 226–35). The vision was inextricably interlaced with the idea of suburb living and proceeded from small service outlets to shopping centres and further on to hypermarkets; from service to self-service; from popping over to various shops for different items, wrapped by the shop assistant, to collecting packaged goods, wheeling them to the checkout and on to the family car. Online shopping has further changed the soundscape of consumption to a more private event from a situation that formerly required interaction with other people and, namely, background music in public (see Uimonen et al. 2017: 11).

4.1 Listener-Consumer: Who Were 'The Audience'?

As the production of background music and the sound design of consumer spaces has developed towards a unifying, branding, and holistic experience, the

Figure 2 Advertising to listener-consumers in Tampere, 1958. The arrival of Father Christmas and the candy mascot Panda by helicopter drew a crowd to the Ratina ground. Regular television broadcasts had started in Finland the same year, gradually transforming locals from unpredictable and easily alienated listener-consumers in public spaces to an audience available most feasibly at home (Photo: Juhani Riekkola, Source: Vapriikki Museum Centre Photo Archives).

spectrum of background music has broadened. Central to this change is the figure of the *listener-consumer*, determined over the decades through increasingly profiled target groups. The ways of describing and analysing the 'audience' vary according to the available technology, music trends, and the level of privacy in spaces accessible for the use of functional music. Finnish texts written by advertising and background music professionals provide an interesting example of this development (see Kilpiö 2016). In the 1940s and 1950s, Finnish listener-consumers were mostly defined in the texts as passers-by in public or semi-public spaces, easily alienated by mistakes such as excess volume, distortion in sound reproduction, or political content. The local urban soundscape carried considerably less musical content than in later decades, which meant that evading functional music was relatively effortless.

For advertising music-makers, television provided access to the listener-consumers' homes – a dramatic change resulting in the professionals considering less the possible alienation and more the music's memorability and general effectiveness. The 1960s listener-consumers appear in the texts as television viewers on one hand and as psychologically susceptible shoppers on the other. Due to the rising standards of living in the country at the time, the 1960s and 1970s writers devoted much attention to the diversifying tastes and musical preferences of listener-consumers. The term 'target group' (*kohderyhmä* in Finnish) was first used in the 1970s. In the later texts, spatial elements of making and experiencing advertising or background music receive less and less attention. They almost disappear, rendering background music as something that is directly communicated from the music content (sound recordings) to the listener-consumer's mind while it was busy making purchasing decisions.

4.2 Muzak and Competitors in Finland: Building a 'Consumers' Republic' with Sound

This section provides a historical timeline of the sonic environment created for listener-consumers with background music in Finnish urban spaces from the 1960s until today. We discuss the characteristics of the background music business in the urban framework. In Finland, business-scale marketing of background music products started in the 1960s, with the increasing importance and contribution of the service sector in the country's economic structure. West-minded men – both individuals and small groups – played an important role in the country's 1950s and 1960s efforts to remain economically open and find ways to prosper in spite of its small size and population (Ojala et al. 2006). Selling music as a production/consumption enhancement tool to the Finnish business administration suited this receptive environment: marketing and publicising was relatively easy. A salesperson for the Finnish Muzak franchising company remembers:

> [S]ome magazines and newspapers got excited, or interested in the idea itself, and wrote articles about it. Then we referred to them and asked, just like a good salesman does nowadays, for an opportunity to come and present this and then they [clients] had one or more people listening to our story (Lindén 2006).

The idea of a subliminal, pleasant way to persuade citizens to produce and consume more fit nicely in the U.S.-derived paradigm of a 'consumer republic'. Combining economic abundance and democratic political freedom – as opposed to the 'impoverishment' of the Soviet system (Cohen 2003: 125–7), the paradigm created trust and faith in mass consumption as a weapon in the Cold War struggles.

In 1960, a Finnish company called Finnestrad acquired the Muzak franchising deal. This was by no means the first instance of background music in city space or in workplaces. For example, an extensive open-air sound system was used for Christmas marketing in 1950 along Aleksanterinkatu, a central shopping street in Helsinki. Next year, the country's oldest and most luxurious department store *Stockmann* introduced its own centrally operated music system for certain sequences within the workday, collaboratively established by the workers' board. Muzak marketing, however, claimed to introduce something new: a package solution of content and technology, curated with 'scientific expertise' (*Helsingin Sanomat* 1961; *Uusi Suomi* 1961). It emphasised the difference between tested, researched background music and 'music as art'. The product was claimed to be essentially different from the 'surrounding music culture', that is, other ways in which people were involved with music. The Muzak selling proposition (the unique benefit offered) was the Stimulus Progression Method, aimed at externally influencing the state of alertness of the employees by changing tempos during the progression of the work day (Lanza 1995: 49).

The franchisee started small but got ample media coverage and growing interest during the 1960s. Finnish businesses were eager to find ways to increase productivity and cost-effectiveness, and subliminal manipulation of human behaviour was promised to deliver results. This created favourable opportunities for Muzak. The company was also active in attempts to widen the vocal possibilities and uses of the PA systems in public spaces, for example an experiment carried out in 1971 in a school in Helsinki, playing background music through the PA system during school days. No positive effects were observed, and teachers' reactions were mainly negative, although pupils were in favour of the music[5].

---

[5] Jarmo Nyström, headmaster of (at the time private) school Pohjois-Tapiolan Yhteiskoulu in a letter to Finnestrad, June 15, 1971.

Finnish listening conventions were also in flux in the 1960s: proponents for contemplative listening and 'serious music' were gradually losing the battle against non-attentive listening and the spreading use of popular music in shared spaces. The triumph of 'scientifically created background tunes', however, soon proved to be temporary as well. In 1981, arguments on Muzak were polarised in the national newspaper *Helsingin Sanomat*. It was questioned whether it was beneficial for the employer to let Muzak reduce the employees' social interaction and chatting. A psychologist interviewed asserted that Muzak had an unfavourable effect on the brain and the central nervous system, a claim denied by Muzak's Finnish sales manager. Allowing the effect might apply regarding [radio] 'programme music', the sales manager argued that Muzak's effect is actually inverted: it is meant to be heard but not listened to in the first place. He also propounded there was a 'surprisingly vast amount of silence sold by Muzak dealers', since their music sequences were followed by a pause of almost equal length. (Uimonen & Kytö 2020.)

Serious rivals for Muzak appeared in the next decade. Musiikki-Fazer, historically the most prominent music publishing company in Finland, established a background music department in 1973. In four years, the company's customer base grew to well over a thousand clients, as the business developed, resulting in a market share of around 60–70 per cent. Musiikki-Fazer represented Philips and its background music system, based on eight-hour-long continuous cassettes (Miettinen 2006). The tapes contained stylistically uniform instrumental and orchestral or choral music, and were based in part on Polygram's catalogue. According to a sticker on one such cassette, the ALLEGRO 747 tape contains 'lively and joyful tunes performed by large orchestras' (ACMEp 2020).

Like Muzak, Musiikki-Fazer relied on the concept of centrally driven music to influence. In public discourse however, the company's representatives had to assure their clients that they did *not* represent 'muzak' (cf. Uimonen & Kytö 2020) – a generalised concept whose image had begun to appear contaminated. Still, the companies competed for the same customers, using partly the same arguments. Musiikki-Fazer's 'alertness music' (*viremusiikki*) was produced by Philips and aimed at affecting the listener's degree of activity. The company stood out from its competitors with its wide selection of music and emphasised the superior sound quality of its products compared to those of its competitors. The system used by Muzak was easy to install, but its sound quality was inferior to magnetic tape, because the music was transmitted via telephone lines. Musiikki-Fazer delivered their cassettes to customers via their own distribution or by mail. The music packages they contained were tailored to each customer's needs and target group. Retail outlets were offered systems that allowed them to record their announcements and combine them with other tape content. (Riikonen 1981: 42; Miettinen 2006.)

The business of background music solutions using separately-tailored musical contents was stifled in the 1970s via new awareness of subliminal control and consumer manipulation, combined with increasing access to music and listening technology via compact cassettes (Kilpiö et al. 2015: 10, 60). Also, instead of employees, background music content began to be aimed increasingly at customers in shops, hotels, and restaurants (Hietanoro 2006). Since the 1980s, subliminal background music was replaced in most commercial environments with *foreground music*, recognisable music repertoire with a more audible character and volume. Today, according to our field work, an overwhelming amount of music encounters in Finnish public city spaces entail music for branding purposes, intended for listening while performing other actions – mostly, consuming. This is particularly true for spaces like large shopping malls, termed 'indoor cities' (Hopkins 1994).

A long-standing source of background and foreground music in restaurants, pubs, bars, and cafés has been the jukebox. This creates an interesting reversion of antecedent technology, since early Muzak had been presented as a contender to the jukebox (Sterne 2003: 189). In Finland, the locations of jukeboxes were medium strength beer licensed establishments, of which a total of 2,716 were founded after the liberalisation of beer sales in 1969. The number of jukeboxes owned by RAY (Finland's Slot Machine Association) peaked in 1977 at almost 3000, at a time when the domestic recording industry was at its strongest. Towards the end of the 1980s, their number fell by two thirds due to the proliferation of cable and satellite television channels and the growth of radio music. (Alko 2022; Muikku 2001: 172.) Music content of the jukeboxes parallels the general transformation of Finnish popular music culture, from the 1970s *iskelmä* (Finnish schlager) and Finnish-language rock called *suomirock* to a widening spectrum of genres including English-language lyrics and media-influenced trends (Nyman 2005). Jukeboxes also helped to disseminate music considered unsuitable, or even banned, by the publicly funded Yleisradio (Finnish Broadcasting Company) due to, for example, allegedly sexual, political, or otherwise dubious lyrics. For their part, jukeboxes thus disrupted and challenged Yleisradio's monopoly. The accessibility of mediated music was further accelerated by the 1980s re-regulation of media.

4.3 Radio Broadcasting and the Digitised Background Music

Terrestrial radio has been by far the most common source of background music in Finland for decades (Partanen et al. 2020). Its popularity at home and in open offices can be explained partly by easy-to-use radio receivers. This competitive edge was consolidated especially after the 1985 media re-regulation, when the first local and commercial stations rearticulated music dissemination but also increased the use of broadcast music in novel contexts. The somewhat conservative Yleisradio was forced to react in fear of losing their audiences. Since its establishment in 1926, Yleisradio (YLE, Finnish Broadcasting Company) had maintained a somewhat paternalistic ethos and enlightening programme policy with a highbrow profile similar to other public broadcasting companies in Europe. The music content consisted predominantly of classical music. Yleisradio's first commercial contender was launched in 1961 when Radio Nord, an offshore station, began broadcasting from the international waters off Stockholm, Sweden. As a consequence, Yleisradio introduced a music programme Sävelradio (Melody Radio) in 1963. The reactive music policy continued twenty years later: in fear of losing their young listeners, Yleisradio launched Rockradio in 1980. (Kemppainen 2001; Kurkela & Uimonen 2009: 138.)

Radio music contents are intertwined with the transformation of music distribution channels, related global trends of the media industry, as well as re-regulation of the media (see Hujanen 2001: 94). The last-mentioned includes changes in radio ownership and music supply within the regulatory framework of the media landscape extending the research scope to techno-logical-economic, historical, socio-cultural and sometimes ideological articulations, discourses, and interactions. When the first commercial and local radios were founded in Finland, the recurring themes in public discussion were radio liberation, breaking of monopolies, media democracy, and how the new radio entrepreneurs would herald this transformation. (Uimonen 2011: 12.)

Yleisradio's radio channels were reorganised in 1990, when the initial enthusiasm in commercial radio stations started to wane. The economic recession of the early 1990s also challenged the future prospects of commercial radio stations. When profiling the channels, Yleisradio paid particular attention to music, since it was considered a suitable strategic tool. Music enabled the broadcaster to reach the desired audience segments and to profile different channels and their programmes' internal structures. (Kemppainen 2001: 148, 152–154, 226–7.)

By the time commercial radio stations were introduced, unobtrusive background music arrangements were replaced in numerous business premises with recordings by original artists intended for listening (Kilpiö 2011: 15). This change was and continues to be influenced by new media technologies and shifts in the ownership of radio stations. Since the early 1990s, the Finnish radio business has become increasingly concentrated in the hands of individual broadcasters and international media houses redefining the target groups and music contents of the radio and also the listeners' relationship with ubiquitous music. (Ala-Fossi 2005; Uimonen 2011.)

In the early 1990s, commercial radio stations and related industries developed computer programs that, combined with multiple CD players, enabled the use of recorded announcements of the studio hosts, and thus the use of unmanned studios and round-the-clock, automated broadcasting. The new software applied in managing background music reflected the digitalisation and emerging automation of music dissemination in general. The background music industry made its first attempts to classify music and programme CD players digitally, too. Furthermore, CD jukeboxes changed later music listening practices profoundly, since they enabled the non-stop playing of music. Jukeboxes provided a continuous stream of less popular performances for the listener, but the hits of the day were available only for a fee. (ACMEi 2021d; Uimonen 2011.)

New innovations in music dissemination were not always considered blessings by background music entrepreneurs. The limited storage capacity of 1990s computer hard drives allowed a practical music quality of compressed mp3-files. After installing a music system to the client's premises, a background music entrepreneur of that time recalls being appalled by its inferior sound quality compared to sound standards set by CDs (ACMEi 2021d).

The post-millennial period in the background music industry can be characterised as an era of changing platforms, with different technologies and background music applications being used in intertwined ways. In the early 2000s, multi-disc CD players were used to provide music for business premises; in the mid-2000s, first attempts were made to control music through computer programming and to transmit music over the internet. (ACMEi 2020a; ACMEi 2022a.) The decision by Finnish telecom operators to sell unlimited 3G packages proved financially disadvantageous to them, however, was not retracted in the transition to 4G and 5G networks. Unlimited data transfer covered most urban areas at the time and the entire country by the 2020s, enabling cheap and accessible mobile streaming and accelerating the ubiquitous use of online music. Companies with a new business logic entered the market, such as Spotify's Soundtrack Your Brand (ex-Spotify Business) with algorithm-based music selection, and Epidemic Sound, which offers 'copyright-free' music to its customers. Background music fees are determined by customer seats or surface area of business premises. Thus, it makes sense, for example, for malls to play music familiar to the end users in their commercial premises, but copyright-free, previously unknown music in their parking garages (ACMEi 2020a).

The public use of radio music or practically any background music is subject to licensing and remuneration. In Finland, background music licences are granted and the collected license fees distributed by Teosto (the copyright society for composers, lyricists, arrangers, and music publishers) and Gramex (the collective management organisation for recorded music). They have been represented since 2016 by their joint venture GT Musiikkiluvat (2022) in handling the sales, marketing, and billing of background music licences. The joint venture underlines that using copyrighted music publicly as agreed ensures that music-makers are remunerated. With radio broadcasting, copyright revenues can be allocated in more detail based on the radio music reports, whereas those of the background music companies are distributed on an estimated basis (GT Musiikkiluvat 2022, ACMEi 2021c). Background music is indeed a lucrative business: in 2019, Teosto received revenues from background music totalling €9.5 million, comparable in size to revenues from concerts and events. Gramex (IFPI Finland) received a total of €9 million from background music.[6]

In promoting background music, GT Musiikkiluvat uses rhetoric that to some extent parallels that of 1970s Muzak, including increasing efficiency and improving atmosphere at workplaces. Unlike Muzak, however, their public discourse explicitly promotes foreground music and underlines individual and collective meanings attached to music by its listeners. Also, instead of using quasi-scientific arguments on music's effects on listeners, GT Musiikkiluvat Oy's website refers to assorted peer-reviewed scholarly literature. Yet another distinction in marketing rhetoric is made by citing interviews of background music clients who characterise royalty-free music somewhat pejoratively as 'elevator music'.

This line of argumentation is also relevant historically: Teosto and the other copyright societies have been active in lobbying for the music-makers' interests and supervising them. In 1962, Teosto had a dispute over revenues with the Finnish Muzak franchisee. The following year, the organisation supervised the use of radio for background music purposes in the Finnish capital, Helsinki, in collaboration with law enforcement (Teosto 2022). Copyright disputes have affected the organisation's public image and been a frequent topic of headlines in the media.

---

[6] In 2019, Teosto's income from background music totalled 9,562,488 euros. Other sources of income, such as concerts and other events, radio, and television, gained 11,360,758 euros, 9,287,581 euros, and 22,290,807 euros respectively. For IFPI Finland, background music income totalled 9,024,336 euros, whereas radio and television programme income totalled 8,899,178 euros (Gramex 2019; Teosto 2019).

4.4 Finland: A Summary

In what follows, we have summarised central cultural, societal and infrastructural characteristics shaping local background music practices in Finland. Traits described previously are condensed here, with added mentions of smaller but relevant factors.

(1) Cultural:

- high overall level of education; relative openness to new technologies and solutions (such as 'Taylorist' use of background music) within the general population
- sonic practices in public spaces: extensive motorisation (however, sounding car horns infrequent)
- radio as a part of the sonic practices – with a significant turning point in 1985, when commercial stations emerged as strong contenders for listeners against the centrally planned, enlightening radio policy of the publicly funded Yleisradio; in a few years independent stations were conglomerated and their music contents streamlined
- extensive use of the Finnish language within the idiosyncratic and extremely popular music genres *iskelmä* (Finnish schlager/pop hit song) and *suomirock* (Anglo-American rock with Finnish lyrics),[7] leading to negotiations in selection for background music playlists
- social communication code with a relatively high tolerance of silence (absence of talk) and quietude[8]
- service culture: a gradual shift in emphasis from errand-running and matter-of-fact behaviour towards nuanced customer service, resulting in increasing demands by employees regarding emotional and sensory labour
- delayed democratisation of restaurant culture; preference of pizzerias and other 'ethnic' restaurants over Finnish ones in the 1960s and 1970s

(2) Societal:

- the influential and proactive position of copyright organisations for composers and musicians
- media re-regulation from the mid-1980s (especially regarding commercial radio – see the previous 'Cultural' section)

---

[7] On the list of best-selling albums of all times in Finland, there are seventeen albums sung in Finnish before Queen's *Greatest Hits 2* (1991), the first album with non-Finnish lyrics. (See www .ifpi.fi/tutkimukset-ja-tilastot/kaikkien-aikojen-myydyimmat/kotimaiset/albumit/, www.ifpi.fi/ tutkimukset-ja-tilastot/kaikkien-aikojen-myydyimmat/ulkomaiset/albumit/.)

[8] See for example Carbaugh et al. (2006).

- relaxing the restrictions and regulations of restaurants and sales of alcoholic beverages, especially in the 1960s and 1970s – for example, decontrolling the locations where medium strength beer was allowed to be sold and served in 1969

(3) Infrastructural:

- late but swift urbanisation, change of economic structure (towards increased importance of the service sector), and consumer society
- prolonged bias in favour of shopping malls and car-centric urban development
- exceptionally centralised grocery trade
- swift adoption of compact cassettes as mainstream listening and *prosuming* technology in the 1970s[9]
- unlimited mobile data packages as a norm from the early 2000s

In the final discussion of this Element, we shall return to these points and characteristics and draft a checklist of questions for future research. In the following three sections, we introduce our empirical approach and results on the aspects of Finnish background music cultures. We proceed from 'factory' (the line of business where background music is produced and compiled) via 'subjects' (service sector employees) and their tactics in the interspace, to the 'consumer' (the end users of city spaces and services in them).

5 Around the Drawing Board: Providing Background Music

This section studies the analysts and designers of the background music industry by considering and contextualising their *agency*. In any environment where music is used, the concept of agency concerns individuals' capacities for action in relation to music or music-related settings. It refers to not only how we do things with music but also how music does something to/for us. Collective music agency can be detected where music is used for structuring social encounters, coordinating bodily action, affirming and exploring collective identity, and knowing the world. (Karlsen 2019: 2–3.)

Embedded in the study of music in culture, agency can be considered to be a socio-musicological and ethnomusicological topic. It can be detected in the various ways in which a society musically defines itself: its taxonomy of music, its ideas of what music does, and in the way it changes its music, relates to,

---

[9] The higher standard of living in other Nordic countries in the 1970s meant a higher degree of saturation in hi-fi listening technology – turntables and reel-to-reel recorders; Finns favoured affordable radio/cassette apparatuses, as well as home taping from contents provided publicly (e.g., radio, music departments of public libraries).

absorbs, and influences other music (Nettl 1983/2005: 12–13). Although music is a 'resource for modulating and structuring the parameters of aesthetic agency' such as feeling, motivation, and desire (DeNora 2000: 53), its use is enabled, restricted, and shaped by social and cultural contexts. A scholarly approach to any contemporary background music company's actions and the agencies of its individual employees should consider the context where music is allegedly being experienced. This is related to the notion that music does not contain any inherent meanings transferrable to its listeners, although it carries an 'immediate threat of history' (Kassabian 2001: 3). For companies providing background music, the contextual reliance is both a blessing and a curse, since it means that music can be controlled to some extent, but total control cannot be achieved.

Agency is related to present-day music culture activities, but also to those aspects of the past that have helped the contemporary music culture to become what it is. Focusing solely on background music companies' current professional environments may not sufficiently explain the existing practices of these companies. They need to be contextualised by charting the employees' previous experience and networks. The contemporary background music industry in Finland is rooted in competence acquired in various sectors of commercial music media, including musicianship, local and commercial radios, disc jockeying, the live music industry, recording studios, and audio engineering. This means that prior to establishing careers in the background music industry, the CEOs and employees already have established networks and experience in retail sales, media, or Finnish music culture in general at their disposal.

By analysing *musicking* (the processes, discourses, and activities related to music) of four diverse Finnish background music companies, it is possible to see how agency is manifest in designing the sonic environments of commercial premises. These conscious choices in sonic environments are constructed with diverse motives by different actors to employ music 'as an ordering material in social life' (DeNora 2000: x). Different background music companies operate in the same field of business, such as in shopping environments or offering music branding services for individual shops and enterprises. Still, there are differences that help to flesh out the multifaceted nature of the industry and the specific areas or fields of expertise that warrant investigation. In one of our recent publications (Uimonen 2022a), agencies of background music companies turned out to be framed quite diversely in contexts of *ownership, clients, music content, overall music profiles, music acquisition, music selection and governing, music evaluation, music platform,* and *client infrastructure.* In what follows, we present examples of how these contexts affect the agencies observable in the companies.

5.1 Background Music Companies

The four background music companies covered in this section operate in the same field of business, but their business environments, clientele, and agencies differ to some extent. Mall Voice plays a key role in building the soundscapes of shopping centres; DjOnline is an experienced developer of music management software; Mood Media[10] operates in Finland, but as a part of an international background music company, which both enables and limits its music selection processes. Bauer Media, unlike other players in the industry, sells generative music to its clients alongside more conventional background music. We interviewed eleven people, ten of whom attended group interview settings at the companies' premises in 2019 and 2020 (ACMEi 2019a; ACMEi 2019b; ACMEi 2020a; ACMEi 2020b). Open-ended questions relating to aforementioned themes were posed to participants, who also brought up topics of their interests such as research and development of music software and client infrastructure.

The Finnish-owned Mall Voice has predominantly shopping malls as clients, and the audible content it provides is composed of voice advertisements and background music used in the hallways. Profiling sonic environments of individual shops or premises is considered more straightforward compared to profiling an entire shopping mall, due to the need to please all end users visiting the premises. According to the company's business philosophy, music should not interfere with shopping, condensed by the interviewee as 'You are not supposed to concentrate on sing-along but to find the nearest optician'. A compilation of 600 to 800 songs characterised as 'non-disturbing' is updated by Mall Voice at least once a month. The principle guiding the company's music selection process is to make potential customers stay longer in the mall. This is partly explained by the fact that the number of out-of-town customers has dropped due to increased online shopping. As a rule of thumb, daily rhythms and language used in song lyrics are taken into consideration in music selection: during daytime, non-Finnish language music content helps Finnish language voice advertisements to stand out. Mall Voice has subcontracted music acquisition to five companies. A suitable subcontractor is selected by Mall Voice personnel and music evaluated from the supplier's ready-made or customised playlists in collaboration with the client, usually represented by shopping mall management. (ACMEi 2019b.)

The principles of quantum modulation are applied to music selection, although the company primarily uses subcontracted and ready-made playlists. Mall Voice strives to distinguish itself from its competitors via its main product –

---

[10] Mood Media Finland merged with Audience First in 2021. In this Element, we call the company Mood Media, since the name was used at the time of our fieldwork.

voice advertising supported by background music. This explains why in Finnish shopping mall environments, speech content overrides and interrupts music content. The process of voice advertisement production in Mall Voice is standardised: a two-minute production time includes the copy reading and audio processing (compression and limiting), resulting in 150 to 250 ads produced per week. According to the studio manager, production time is limited due to the relatively large number of completed ads, which are then updated on the client's sound system. The amount of audio advertising included in Mall Voice contracts means voice advertisements are not only played between music tracks. Background music is faded out before a voice advertisement is played, and after the ad, the overall sound level is automatically restored. (ACMEi 2019b.)

DjOnline (ACMEi 2020a), a locally owned background music company, operates with a different clientele and business logic compared to Mall Voice. It provides music for various enterprises and actively researches and develops software for music selection applications. The company's personnel characterised their line of work as providing music for 'public premises' where different products or services are offered. Instead of music genres, specific artists are used as reference points, especially when clients may be uncertain what they are looking for. Individual playlists are evaluated by client feedback and customised accordingly. Unlike background music targeted to a wider audience (e.g. in a shopping mall environment), DjOnline's tailored music selection takes advantage of the alleged personal and collective meanings attached to songs and music genres. DjOnline personnel outline music profiles for smaller enterprises such as bars and restaurants in accordance with their customers' music tastes. Music, including record companies' new releases and the occasional hand-picked songs from company employees' personal analogue record collections, is acquired by uploading it to the company's server. (ACMEi 2020a.) For selecting, controlling, and evaluating music, DjOnline's personnel use the company's own categorisation and evaluation system, with parameters such as tempo, year of publication, language, length, and whether the music is considered suitable for background or foreground use. The parameters supersede a time-consuming song-by-song compiling of the playlists.

The nature of the background music business and its end product has also transformed from the era of functionally arranged music. The business logic of contemporary background music companies is based on the dissemination of music and on the background music companies' professional skills in selecting and categorising music. It is more akin to the business logic of a commercial radio station or a gig promoter than of producers of music content.

A recurring topic in the interviews was technological and infrastructural constraints restricting professional sound design and how these issues should be solved when designing and constructing malls. The DjOnline personnel strongly criticised shopping mall *infrastructure* and its design, especially the use of outdated or inferior quality loudspeakers.

> Those highly paid interior designers with huge salaries . . . they think about colours and they think about furniture and then comes this Excel guy, who decides to save ten euros from each loudspeaker of the emergency audio system. After that it is practically impossible to make good sound design. (ACMEi 2020a)

The emergency audio systems' mid-range loudspeakers are considered suitable for announcements, but they are poorly suited to some music genres. The audio system dramatically emphasises the frequency of brass instruments. The personnel recounted a case where, because of this feature, their client's hopes of specific up-tempo music for specific parts of the mall remained unfulfilled: when volume was adjusted in accordance with the horn section, the speech content, such as announcements and advertisements, was practically inaudible. On the other hand, in some premises, the audibility of background music was poor due to loud sound levels of refrigerators and digital slot machines (ACMEs/Kk 2020).

Thus, musicking in the background music context expands to questions of listening and understanding not only music content but also the material surroundings of where (and how) music is distributed and experienced. A representative of a major background music distributor reminisced on these challenges already in the 1980s, a time when business was expanding from workplaces to public premises. Music was intended to mask, for example, the sound sources of restaurants, which required an education process: new clientele were deliberately advised *not* to pay attention to the music. (Hietanoro 2006.) The interaction of music, listener, and place was intentionally transformed when clients were encouraged to dishearken background music.

The multinational company Mood Media (ACMEi 2020b) also follows the logic of quantum modulation practices. The personnel have vast resources at their disposal, and they follow the general outlines of their international music selection policies. An *overall music profile* is tailored to the clients' needs – a process that often includes mapping the business premises and target groups depending on the brand's image or customer traffic flow. As pointed out by one research participant, by selling a product with jazz or classical music, 'you can probably ask for a higher price than you can ask with basic pop music' that's available on commercial radio 'to anyone who wishes to listen to it'. The company's international music resources and music expertise of various genres and languages are available for employees in Finland. In practice, this means that music acquisition, selection, and control are carried out to a large extent in collaboration with the conglomerate's international personnel 'tagging' songs (categorising music with different parameters). Use of algorithms in music selection in their line of business was not considered proper: 'It takes between ten and fifteen minutes for a client to visit a shop ... This equals about five songs, and there is no chance to do it well if you let some machine randomly select music with similar rhythm' (ACMEi 2020b).

At Mood Media (ACMEi 2020b), the company's music designer evaluates artists, lyrics, and even solitary words in the context of client needs, labelling a song with lyrics deemed dubious or negative as improper in the company's software. The practice underlines the nature of selecting background music for public premises: a song suitable for a nostalgic rock radio channel is considered improper for a waiting room 'if you are about to see an oncologist'. Algorithm-based playlists used by online music services were criticised due to their unpredictability: Sting's 'Englishman in New York' is a 'classic' and could be categorised as popular music of a certain decade for a certain demographic, but the song's dynamic arrangement makes it unsuitable for background music compilations for public premises. Selecting music is framed by cultural norms and language aspects. Some artists are banned from Mood Media playlists – they simply cannot be selected by the personnel even if requested by clients. The company's software is equipped with specific colour codes for categorising music. No four-letter words are allowed, nor songs containing lyrics that *might* remotely sound like these in a noisy environment. On the other hand, Finnish Mood Media employees code domestic releases in accordance with company policies, which allows selecting some English-language songs from Finnish releases that might be considered inappropriate in English-speaking countries. This freedom of agency was described by an employee as follows: 'I am able to retrieve songs ... with lyrics including where you're "high" referring to that you're stoned or in a good mood. Some U.S. brands are sensitive even to that' (ACMEi 2020b).

Bauer Media offers generative music (produced by software using parameters to generate ambient-like sonic streams, with a logic similar to videogame music). An overall music profile for generative music is delivered for them by Sound Agency in London, UK. According to Sound Agency (2014), 'generative soundscapes are relatively association-free', ever-changing, and capable of emulating natural or urban soundscapes or musical styles. They are typically played at an ambient level, 'operating at the subconscious level rather than being foreground sound'. Potential environments suitable for generative music can be any public space with unpleasant sounds or noise, such as train and metro stations, airports, and shopping malls, that are not suitable for background music. Bauer Media considers that generative music can be used for making a place more sonically pleasant, to make people more peaceful, or to quicken their pace. Clothing stores with young employees, who may 'need to be activated' with music, are not necessarily among the product's end users. (ACMEi 2019a.)

Resembling Muzak marketing rhetoric halfway through the twentieth century, Bauer Media interviewee characterised generative music by juxtaposing it with background music – or any music, for that matter. The definitions relate to a general understanding that generative music is distinctively something Western popular music is *not*, supported by the argument that generative music lacks structures such as repetition and choruses: 'We produce soundscapes – or our device produces soundscapes ... You never know what is going to happen next' (ACMEi 2019a). This definition of soundscape bears little resemblance to the concept's scholarly use (Schafer 1977). Instead, it is used discursively for advertising and product differentiation from the company's other products, such as audio branding and radio advertising, of which the latter is predominantly framed by meticulously compiled playlists of well-known popular music (see next section).

Generative music is evaluated by feedback from clients, whose employees have sometimes described it as 'boring' – especially where it has replaced the foreground music used earlier (ACMEi 2019a). When evaluated in the context of individual and collective meanings attached to music, the comment of 'boring music' holds true. It also makes yet another explanation plausible. Since 'music refers to other music' and 'music in the mainstream uses musical codes to convey a mood or idea' (Kassabian 2001: 51), it seems that generative music runs the risk of not being able to refer to something even vaguely familiar to the listeners or their expectations.

> Yeah, this has variation – the stuff that gets played on radios and so on. We had an experiment where every other day a sort of tinkling was played and then again ordinary music. It was just awful [the interviewee made a weary gesture] and the customers were like [here, the interviewee glowered]. That was terminated, and we gave feedback. (ACMEf/Joensuu)

Another analogy between generative music and music provided by Muzak is the absence of lyrics. The social content of music represented by lyrics and familiar melodies transfers the past to the present (Husch 1984; 131–2; Kilpiö 2013: 237), which enables workers to manage their time and use music as a 'mental outlet' from monotonous work. This function of music seems to be missing from generative 'soundscapes': they continue the 'intentional decentering and distribution of subjectivity by musical means' (Anderson 2015: 819) inherent in Muzak and other mood music content. Generative music challenged background music by stripping cultural meanings attached to music content listened to in public places. It remains to be seen whether its parameters are capable of conveying subtle, culturally specific meanings to music by combining melodic fragments, keys, modes, intervals, and so on – familiar to its listeners but not so obvious as to be actualised at the level of the personal meanings attached to existing songs or instrumental music.

Bauer Media stated that they have installed microphones in 'public premises to listen to noise levels' in order to help to adjust the volume of background music. This automatic adjustment of the sonic environment is planned to be carried out in the future with the help of external data such as weather, cash register receipts, number of customers in premises, or even facial recognition to provide information for the system on parameters such as age and gender of customers. (ACMEi 2019a.)

Legal and ethical questions may yet induce stumbling blocks for the use of data collected from various sources by digital technology in service of the background music industry. The idea itself parallels larger trends of utilising external data in music selection processes. The digital music streaming service Spotify patented a technology that will allow the analysis of users' voices and then suggest songs based on their 'emotional state, gender, age, or accent'. This would allow observing not only users' emotions but also their environment using machine listening technology. (Savage 2021.) The General Data Protection Regulation sets out requirements for companies and organisations on collecting and managing personal data, applying it to organisations in the European Union and organisations outside the EU that target people living in the EU (2021). This may suggest that music's public use is becoming the subject of data protection, which is monitored and regulated at both the national and European levels.

When music affects social or commercial agency, the control over music is a source of social and/or commercial negotiation of power. This is manifested in affordances constructed in various commercial spaces, supporting various agencies available to customers. Music or any other sounds can also be used to signify explicitly non-democratic issues, or to help maintain social inequality – a policy that would be hard to accept in any other form of city planning (Sterne 2013: 135).

5.2 Radio Content as Background Music

In this section, we focus on the background uses and features of radio content by analysing the operating principles and programming logic behind the audible outcome. In public urban space, radio programming content competes with other media content. Commercial and publicly funded radio music can be characterised as ubiquitous. Whether intended or not, radio music returns the listeners' affects and past experiences to everyday listening situations. This is complemented by the present-day topics selected and commented on by radio hosts.

Terrestrial radio stations provide most of the background music in Finland. A 2020 report by the copyright organisation Teosto (Partanen et al. 2020: 4–7, 25) found that background music derived from terrestrial radio is most often listened to in shops, barbershops, restaurants, taxis, and sports facilities. Radio's share as background music had increased since 2019 (from 66 per cent to 68 per cent), whereas background music services were used by only 12 per cent of the companies. Finnish Broadcasting Company YLE's radio channels are most common in taxis (55 per cent) and restaurants (34 per cent), while commercial radio channels are most listened to in fitness centres (96 per cent).

Radio channels and background music companies can be approached as cultural industries referring to producers and distributors of different forms of culture, competing with each other for the same resources. These include limited pools of disposable consumer income, advertising revenue, consumption time, and skilled creative and technical labour (Hesmondhalgh 2019: 16). Drawing from available research on the culture industry, the music industry and its products can be interpreted as a means of organising consumers' leisure time and thus facilitating reproductive labour for the sake of profit (cf. Horkheimer & Adorno 2008). Radio programming pursues this through music selection that aims to regulate not only the listeners' leisure time but also time spent at work. Assumption of music and speech content as mood regulators of workers can be detected in the advertising discourses of radio stations. The choice of music and the nature of the radio hosts' parlance have features similar to the Taylorist understanding of workplace well-being ('Every weekday from 10 a.m. to 2 p.m. on NRJ's weekdays, René is by your side and sees to it that you can make it through the day!'; Kilpiö 2005: 11).

Analysis of radio programme contents as a companion for everyday life should not be restricted only to music. Individual songs, artists, or genres are elements in the recognisable overall audible image of the radio that provides the backdrop for music. This image, often called channel sound, is composed of music, jingles, advertisements, speech content, and the tempo of the channel. Also, broadcasting and sound editing technologies such as compression are used to smooth out the loud and quiet parts of speech and music to make the content more consistent – another reason for considering the channel sound as a whole whenever aiming for an expedient analysis. (Uimonen 2011: 31–2, 135.) Contemporary radio channel sound and the related music selections are in some respects comparable to the business strategies of background music companies.

It is relatively easy to identify similarities between the music and speech content of radio and that of the background music industry, for the simple reason that it is possible to listen to their ubiquitous music content in a wide variety of contexts (see Sterne 2013: 124).

In the 1990s, the Finnish commercial radio industry prioritised channel sound over its components, such as individual music tracks, artists, or even show hosts. Playlists and broadcast clocks[11] were adopted to control each broadcasting hour with an attempt to follow the listeners' daily rhythm (Uimonen 2017), resembling the Stimulus Progression Method. However, radio programming cannot be simply placed on the historical continuum of the background music industry: a quarter-hour of music and an equal time of silence would obviously be unthinkable in radio stations. Nevertheless, the music selection process of contemporary format radio carries similarities to quantum programming, aiming for consistent and non-disturbing music content.

The most listened channels for background music are currently the publicly funded Yleisradio's Radio Suomi (Radio Finland) and the only nationwide commercial station, Radio Nova, founded in 1997 and now owned by the multimedia-conglomerate Bauer Media (Uimonen 2022b). The two channels differ in terms of not only ownership but also their music content and music selection processes. Radio Suomi is guided by current principles of public broadcasting. Characterised by its management (ACMEi 2021a) as 'the radio of the people', it aims to sound familiar and safe, appealing to all Finnish listeners. Radio Suomi's music director preselects music, which is then evaluated in panels consisting of members of the staff working with the company's music content. Radio Nova, according to its advertising slogan, broadcasts 'classics and the coolest new releases', effectively, hit songs. Its policies are dictated by AC (adult contemporary) format radio. (ACMEi 2021b.) The music content must appeal to the music tastes of their target audience (from 25 to 45 years of age) and therefore hits must be played evenly from different eras and decades. New songs are selected and added to the playlist by the music director or producer. Unlike Radio Suomi, Radio Nova tests its music content online on a weekly basis with the help of over 100 radio listeners.

The content of the stations was selected for our research based on its popularity and analysed by data provided by the National Audiovisual Institute. The primary data consisted of music content during the peak hours (8 a.m. to 6 p.m.) on Wednesday, 8 September 2021, and the speech content of both channels for one hour (8–9 a.m.) on the same day. Data selection was based on the fact that

---

[11] A broadcast clock is a template displaying the radio's hourly format in a graphical representation of a clock, helping segments such as news and commercials be repeated every hour at given times (Wiki 2023).

the morning hour is considered to define radio listening throughout the day and thus perceived as particularly important by radio broadcasters (ACMEi 2021b). The primary data was supported by secondary data from thematic interviews with Radio Suomi and Radio Nova representatives (ACMEi 2021a; ACMEi 2021b), clarifying radio programming, speech content, and especially music selection processes. The analysis revealed that during the peak listening hours (6 a.m. to 6 p.m.), publicly funded Radio Suomi aired a total of 65 individual songs, of which 70 per cent had Finnish-language lyrics. The music aired was released between 1960 to 2020 and 58 per cent of music content was released after 2000. New releases covered 21 per cent of the music content. There was no recurring airplay of individual songs. Established Finnish artists such as J. Karjalainen, Jarkko Martikainen, and Pepe Willberg were broadcast along with non-Finnish releases such as Anastacia, Cher, Hot Chocolate, and Neil Young.

Commercial Radio Nova was formatted slightly differently. During the peak listening hours (6 a.m. to 6 p.m.), Radio Nova aired a total of 102 individual songs, of which 23 per cent had Finnish-language lyrics. Three-fourths of the music aired was released after 2000. New releases covering 20 per cent of the music content were aired recurringly during the peak listening hours. Radio Nova did broadcast Finnish artists, but the majority of music content was composed of Anglo-American releases and established artists such as the Backstreet Boys, Ed Sheeran, Enrique Iglesias, and Roxette.

On a general level, music programming of both Radio Suomi and Radio Nova relies mainly on English-language pop, Finnish iskelmä, suomirock, and adult oriented rock. However, Radio Suomi broadcasts domestic music genres and artists more frequently than its competitor. With its music content released since the 1960s, Radio Suomi seemingly offers more variety to the listeners. (Uimonen 2022b.) This is partly explained by the *Act on Yleisradio Oy* (Finlex 1993/2017) ('versatile and comprehensive television and radio programming ... for all citizens under equal conditions') but more likely due to the 2019 restructuring of the channel's programme content.

Approaching radio music content from the perspective of the background music industry production culture, we can interpret radio content as a compilation of functional sounds: it has a clear, predetermined purpose, place, and context of use, chosen by those who decide on the content. To fully understand this, we need to clarify who the alleged listeners of the channels are and in which contexts and at what time of the day music is supposedly listened to. The National Radio Survey – a joint research project of Yleisradio and commercial radio stations based on participants' listening diaries, states that in 2021, Finns listened to radio approximately 2 hours and 28 minutes daily. Most listening happened at 9 a.m. on workdays, when radio channels reached

1.1 million listeners. The weekly reach of radio channels was 4.4 million listeners. (Brun 2021.)

Both Radio Suomi's and Radio Nova's programming is based on listeners' daily, weekly, and yearly rhythms. News rotation is more frequent on weekdays, compared to more entertaining weekend content. Music content is planned according to weekdays and determined by the station's broadcast clock. Radio Suomi is listened to predominantly in cars, workplaces, and homes, by elderly listeners with button-equipped car radios and easy-to-use table radios. The somewhat uniform radio culture is changing, however, since fewer listeners are commuting at 8 a.m. and 4 p.m. (ACMEi 2021a). In addition, Radio Nova's content director (ACMEi 2021b) underlined that the increase of remote work has changed the daily rhythms of the listeners. Radio Nova also noted the importance of collective listening in the workplace in terms of using radio for background music: the station's afternoon programming is more entertainment-based in comparison to its news-packed mornings.

Transforming media policies and changes in dissemination of mediated music have affected the programme planning of radio stations. Streaming services have increased the supply of music to the extent that they are challenging radio stations in the competition for audiences. Radio Suomi (ACMEi 2021a) and Radio Nova (ACMEi 2021b) no longer consider music content their primary means of competition; in recent years, they have both added speech content due to increased popularity of on-demand music services. The popularity of podcasts has also affected programme planning, increasing speech content on the radio. Consequently, the role of radio hosts was emphasised on commercial channels, whereas publicly funded channels will be relying on curated and journalistic content.

Drawing from recent developments in the Finnish media environment, it can be concluded that instead of focusing specifically on ubiquitous radio *music* content, we should pay attention to ubiquitous radio content in general. Listeners' daily rhythms are increasingly driven by not only music but also speech, including dialogue between the audience and the radio hosts, who are adjusting their voices according to the type of station for which they work, targeting their content to Andersonian (2020: 74) imagined communities (Lacey 2013: 93–94). Furthermore, radio channels bring yet another layer to the topic of varied audio content as background music: a multiple understanding and overlapping notion of time. Radio speech content happens in the present, commenting on topical issues and interacting with the world. By airing previously released music, radio stations invite their listeners back to the past, with music-related memories as part of their listening experiences.

The changing role of the radio host is linked to the increased supply of mediated music, which makes it challenging for a radio station to compete for the listener's time only with music content. However, the same digital platforms that challenge radio content also enable radio channels to invent novel ways of communicating with their audiences by expanding the policies of terrestrial radio broadcasting (Uimonen 2022b). Both Radio Suomi and Radio Nova have established a symbiotic relationship with streaming services: they publish their content on Spotify and link their websites to Spotify's platform. Texts and images (still and moving) as well as sounds previously attached to a specific medium now converge on different digital platforms and even live music venues and festivals, all owned by an individual company. An artist or a performance is given exposure through all channels provided by the media conglomerate. Thus, selecting new releases to radio playlists evidently connects to other means of music distribution. This relationship between an artist and a media company can be established at a very early stage (Uimonen 2020a: 267). An artist recording potential hit songs in the studio might consult the advice of radio music directors even before the song is in its final form – a procedure likely to influence radio music content and, eventually, background music. Both publicly funded and commercial radio music directors agree that it is more advisable to spend money reserved for broadcasting remuneration on possible all-time favourites and more enduring performances rather than 'one-hit wonders'. For further contextualising the background music industry, media convergence needs to be considered.

6 Behind the Till: Background Music as a Tool for Service Work

In this section, we examine the views of service sector employees on 'working with music' as well as its impact on well-being at work and during leisure time. For businesses providing and buying background music for service workplaces and commercial premises, the rationale for it is explicitly economic: increasing sales. The most frequent *listeners* of background music, however, are employees such as salespeople, waiters, security guards, and hotel workers: during their workday, they hear an average of eight hours of music. In most cases, they do not get to choose the music themselves. This raises questions regarding the position of employees in relation to background music and what it is like to work with music. In terms of soundscape research, they constitute the functional acoustic community (Kytö 2013: 22) best placed to articulate the meanings of their environments.

Compared with the rest of Europe, Finnish working life is characterised by 'high levels of trust, low levels of tension between management and employees, good participation possibilities for employees, and developed social dialogue in workplaces' (Kauhanen & Nevavuo 2021: 2). Besides varying degrees of power to influence the practices of music selection, workers have different ways of influencing and adapting to their working environment, and they apply different tactics in doing so (DeNora 2000: 137; de Certeau 2013). They also work with music as a spatial element that, among other things, can function as a tool for them.

While the relationship between paying customers and background music as an element of service facilities has been relatively well studied (see e.g. Sterne 1997; Ranta 2005; Stenbäck 2016; Kontukoski & Uimonen 2019), less academic attention has been devoted to our focus in this section – the relationships between service workers and the music of their workspaces. Payne, Korczynski, and Cluley (2017) focused their analysis of extensive field data on the factors influencing the experience of background music and the consequences of these factors for the employee. They outlined a four-part model for the role of music in customer service work. The model places the musical environment on a scale from alienating to satisfying, and customer contact on a scale from purely positive to unambiguously negative. Positive communication between worker and client in an alienating musical environment can resemble a 'co-conspirators' encounter, whereby the worker confirms or implies that they, like the client, find the background music distasteful. Negative customer contact in an alienating musical environment, on the other hand, often leads to a deliberate 'tuning out'. In the latter case, the employee alleviates the alienation not by sharing the experience, but rather by tolerating both stimuli, the annoying client and the tiresome music. On the other hand, if the employee finds the musical environment satisfying or indeed enjoyable, an opportunity arises to either bridge for sociality through music in the context of positive customer contact or to mitigate the debilitating effect of negative customer contact by focusing on the music as 'a haven from customers' (Payne et al. 2017: 1423–4).

A recent Swedish study (Carlén 2018) approached the issue from the perspective of well-being at work and improvement of working environments. Using a multiple-choice questionnaire, the study looked at how employees (n = 2127) perceived music – or the lack of it – in relation to their work environment, their involvement and level of knowledge in music selection processes, and the impact of these factors on their experience of music. The survey strongly recommended commissioning risk assessments in workplaces and the systematic inclusion of music in workplace improvement efforts.

In our study of over 800 Finnish service employees' views on music in the workplace (Kilpiö & Kytö 2021), we found the link between well-being at work and background music only tenuously linked to the employees' personal musical preferences or opportunities for administering the precise musical content in the workplace. Far more significant were the opportunities to create one's own agency in relation to workplace music – ideally through professional identity – and the meaningful use of sonic affordances in client interactions. Professional agency seems to play an important role in work-related well-being. This also came up during field work: a café worker explained that she could select music by choosing the radio channel, but personal preference was not a priority. According to her: 'Yes, I can choose the channel myself, but I can't play rock music [which I would prefer] because it's not a rock venue – you have to think about the customers' (ACMEf/Joensuu). A service sector workplace transforms the meaning of music into a professional one for the employees, relegating their personal musical relationships to secondary roles.

In our field material, some service sector employees also questioned the sonic architecture in which music is situated in the workplace. Their answers described the different (sonic) factors influencing the way music is heard, and the experience of space, embodiment, and, through this, comfort and well-being at work. They also reported on efforts to change their sonic environments. Based on our empirical evidence, focusing on background music alone, without taking into account the rest of the sonic environment, produces uncontextualised results. After all, background music is often motivated by its capacity to mask other sounds and to guarantee privacy in customer service situations; it is added to any commercial space largely in relation to the existing sonic setting: to mask other sounds or silence or to emphasise the ambience, décor, and features of the sales articles.

The role adopted by the employee in the construction of the soundscape is an indication of their agency. They can enhance their well-being at work by observing how the soundscape functions and how favourable conditions for it could be promoted. This idea of 'diagnosing' the good qualities, that is, the 'health' of the soundscape (Amphoux 1993), involves reinforcing those qualities within the soundscape that are deemed positive, increasing the awareness about attributes related to well-being to those who work in the soundscape, observing spatial and temporal sonic characteristics, and considering the sonic construction of social interaction. It also refers to protecting spaces from noise, that is, regulating and controlling sound sources and providing sound insulation. The worker, alone or with colleagues, can seek workable sound solutions if they see opportunities to do so. However, it is often seen as too complex, expensive, or requiring a major infrastructure effort. Moreover, this perceived extra work is often outside their formal job description. One respondent to the online survey stated unequivocally: 'I am a gig worker and it is not my job to criticise the working environment of my clients'

(ACMEs/PAM 2021b). Of the respondents to the online survey, 18 per cent had not discussed music with colleagues at all. Workers seemingly often approach the health of the environment with either indifference, powerlessness, or the general idea of the soundscape as inherently flawed and therefore incurable, remediable only temporarily. This was also reflected in the comments by several interviewees that discussing music at the workplace was labelled as 'complaining' and thus best avoided.

In its simplest form, maintenance of the workplace soundscape happened by replacing what was playing with music of collective or an individual employee's choice. Several restaurant employees reported a practice of switching to more upbeat 'own music' for the evening's finishing touches after customers had left. Another routine maintenance measure was adjusting the background music volume. Just under half of the respondents to the online survey said they could adjust the volume of the music directly from the sound system. Understandably, this seems to be the practice in the hospitality sector, where patrons spend more time in the premises and often also view music as an element of their customer experience. One in four respondents – mostly from the retail sector – reported they could not control the volume (ACMEs/PAM 2021).

Playing music at the lower limit of the hearing threshold, that is, very quietly, is a tactic used by some workers to mask noise, for example, from air conditioning and escalators, as we observed at the *Koskikeskus* shopping centre in Tampere.[12] Such tactics of background music use render audible only some of its frequencies and rhythmic elements, and possibly the singing voice. In some shops, turning down the volume to a level barely audible was tacitly agreed among the staff for music not liked, hoping the manager would fail to find out the business was paying for streaming non-audible music. In shops staffed by a single person, it was also possible to turn the radio on or off according to the number of customers entering the shop, and to thus control the customer space completely autonomously (ACMEs/Kk 2020a). Non-access to controlling the volume increases the laboriousness and effort required for *sensory labour* – the active process of domesticating and adapting to the sensory environment – especially in customer service situations. Pricking up one's ears tires and stresses customers as well.

In soundscape descriptions, the describer typically ignores the sounds they produce, that is, the self as a sound source. This was also the case in our field

---

[12] Tampere is the third largest city in Finland, with a university and a population of about a quarter million. A playlist of all songs heard by our research team during the March 2020 Koskikeskus fieldwork week can be found here: https://open.spotify.com/playlist/1aGeG1nxe3X5CmMwEnteSo?si=7f2685dc82eb412e.

material, in spite of the fact that sales work, restaurant catering, and other customer service labour is very much about talking. Respondents played an important role in producing the sonic environment of their workplace themselves, by not only speaking but also doing other chores emitting sound (carrying and shelving products, pushing carts, washing dishes, setting up tables, walking, using machines, etc.). Background music was described by the respondents as an element in a sometimes dense soundscape, the 'healthiness' of which was influenced at a worker level by two factors: the use of headphones and overlapping music.

Of the respondents to the online survey, one in five reported headphone use, for creating a personal sound space within the customer service premises, for both isolation (e.g. dishwashing shift with noise-cancelling headphones) and communicating with other employees (e.g. radiophones used by vendors and security guards). The use of a headset in one ear and a microphone on a shirt collar was common: 'We have to wear an earpiece where someone is always chattering' (ACMEs/PAM 2021c). These respondents were connected to overlapping audio infrastructures during their working hours, which could prove challenging when their speech work had to be placed in the context of the rest of the soundscape: a person speaking into the microphone could not know whether the other users could concentrate on listening at a given moment.

Our field data repeatedly mentions overlapping music. In the Koskikeskus centre, for example, several streams of background music could be heard simultaneously in the front areas of stores with open entrances. In such cases, employees reported feeling more comfortable deeper in the store, where the hallway music did not carry over. 'Fortunately, the shop's own music covers the shopping centre's own elevator music [i.e. hallway music] quite well' (ACMEs/Kk 2020b). When events took place in the lobby of the shopping centre, the sound equipment and the volume of the hallway music increased. Employees responded to the increase in sound sources by adjusting the volume of the background music in their shops or turning it off completely. Sometimes playing overlapping music in shops was a subversive tactic to drown out hallway music seeping in. Maintaining aural and musical hygiene was also part of the job of the security guards. Specific management situations of overlapping music arose when young people spending their leisure time in the shopping centre played music through their own mobile phones and Bluetooth speakers. These rare situations produced unwanted, disturbing music (as far as the shopping centre management was concerned), and usually ended with security guards intervening to remove the unwanted sound sources.

Survey responses also highlighted the importance of using music and other forms of listening for well-being in the workplace. Employees might listen to their own playlists, podcasts, and audio books on their headphones during quiet times, or a hairdresser might take dance steps to the radio music during morning cleaning. Workers with job descriptions that did not include speaking to customers could be in touch with friends and family by phone on a very personal basis during their shift, or listen to music of their choice. As far as we can see, these types of agencies had a strong impact on the social well-being of the workers. After all, each service worker has their own musical world, their own personal listening and hearing limitations (with sensory sensitivities, hearing impairments, musical preferences, etc.).

Sometimes the responsibilities of taking care of the sonic environment are not evenly distributed among workers. This is due to their being seen as secondary in tasks given, and for that reason difficult to identify and negotiate among employees. In light of our data, it also appears that in work environments where workers are not given the opportunity to act on its music or sounds, there is a lack of common vision of a 'healthy' soundscape. The understanding of the appropriateness and functionality of the environment may also differ between the employee and the shopkeeper. In our view, opportunities for communal building of meaningful and inspiring acoustic spaces are missed by assuming that everyone manages their musical and sonic relationships on their own and finds isolated tactics to adapt to a soundscape determined by the sales strategies of the workplace. Understanding the functional acoustic community as a collective space for negotiation also allows for the sharing of responsibility for the burdensome sensory labour.

6.1 Adult Novelty Stores: Normalising 'Embarrassing Products' Sonically

It is common knowledge that the balance between aspects of background music use varies considerably depending on the area of business, space, target group, etc. However, it is also possible to recognise areas where music is employed to reduce rather than induce the consumers' impulsivity and affectivity. Among these are the premises that sell so-called *embarrassing products* (see e.g. Dahl et al. 2001; Andersson 2016; Ringler et al. 2022), such as, for example, sex toys, contraceptives, or pharmaceuticals. Facilities for purchasing such products aim to ensure the listener-consumer's mindset remains within everyday reality, and the senses are not pulled into a drift towards erotic reality (see Davis 1983: 45) or other altered realities such as those associated with substance abuse. The following short summary of our case study on Finnish adult novelty stores

(Kilpiö 2023) reveals how crucial zoning the patrons' impulses may prove in managing the sonic environment at business premises. The study was based on interviews, field work diaries (ACMEf/Sex), and survey results from Lahti.[13]

In the studied context – downtown sex shops in a mid-sized Finnish city – the main principle in planning the commercial space was *ordinariness*: the experience was sonically linked to everyday reality, and altered realities were kept in check. Affective resonance, that is, the transmitting of sexual affect to the listener-consumer through sound (see Kytö 2016: 3, 11), is considered undesirable in sex shop premises. Typically for Finnish music culture, susceptibility to affective resonance was warded off in the shops via utilising a commercial radio channel[14] broadcasting easy-going musical and verbal content. As the most frequent local background music source, it was deemed most effective in creating a familiarity effect and conveying mundanity in terms of the soundscape. A store employee described the role of music radio content:

> It gives people time to hang out there [between the shelves]. It's like a sort of cloak of invisibility. I mean if it's really quiet here, I can hear all the rustling and everything that goes on over there, so they probably won't dare touch anything or look at stuff – now my attention is away from there. (ACMEi 2022b)

Customer service staff in sex shops pointed out that shoppers wished to mask the sounds of their own conversations and product browsing, as well as to establish the general atmosphere of their stay in the zone of normality – as a part of everyday reality. Regardless of their sector, those working in customer service professions clearly have a capacity to recognise several features of commercial sonic environments, with or without background music. One of these features is the potential of silence to cause social discomfort and an off-putting (in R. Murray Schafer's terms, centrifugal) sound environment. In their survey responses (ACMEs/PAM 2021), employees used terms such as 'uncomfortable', 'awkward', 'annoying', 'embarrassing', and 'oppressive'.

The shops did not target certain customer segments with their sonic solutions; rather, they held up the impression of sexual pleasure as something that belonged to all adults and could be safely discussed with the store employees. This might produce boring or centrifugal sonic environments for sex shop customers with a more adventurous or sensation-seeking mindset, but the businesses studied prioritised a more mainstream customer base. Whereas impulsivity and affectivity could enhance sales in most other commercial

---

[13] Lahti is a university town in Southern Finland with approximately 120,000 inhabitants.
[14] The channels mentioned were Suomirock, Hitmix, Ysäri, Nostalgia, Radio Rock, and Radio City.

premises, here the sheltering everydayness of radio was appreciated, and its daily schedule of news, music, and talk content was tapped into for customised alienation. The role of music in back room private shows – and hence the range of music played there – was altogether different from that of the adult novelty product premises. An important finding was that those working in service professions recognised the sonic nature of distinguishable zones, and they did so across different sectors. In the case of the sex shop back rooms, music was an essential element within the tailor-made experience, chosen and controlled by the performers. Personalised by them in each customer contact they built, music was a primary element of the show, defining its characters, atmosphere, and emphasis. The aim was to provide customers with fantasy-leaning experiences, and thus in their introductory texts or in booking situations at the premises, the performers sought to convey the most essential aspects of these experiences to potential clients. As part of their professional skills, staff in the shops recognised the aural affordances and the differences that defined spaces. (Kilpiö 2023: 37–8.)

A study on the British Sh! sex shop chain is exceptional in that it describes the role of music in the general 'stage setting' of the stores together with the physical concept. The researchers describe the music and customer focus of the Sh! stores as follows:

> Classical music, soulful female singers, and 'out and proud' lesbian bands act as the orchestra in the dramatic performance in *Sh!*. This eclectic approach to music appears to signal vigilant attention to non-alienation of specific groups of women and is consistent with the owner's wish to embrace diversity. (Malina & Schmidt 1997: 356)

The design of the chain's premises aims towards relaxed service encounters, allowing for a lingering browsing experience, and facilitating communication between customers who do not know each other.

The observations of different 'zones' of reality (e.g. from everyday to erotic) and the affordances to diverse experiences are both relevant for the study of background music cultures. We see them as worthwhile considerations in research settings also outside the scope of embarrassing products and otherwise sensitive consumer experiences. Exploring the applicability of zones for research – as constructed spaces between the general store and aisle sound atmospheres and the 'microspheres' of individualised headscapes – can prove fruitful for analysing the 'calibrated architectures of affect' (Anderson 2015: 812, 816). Developing zone analysis further, preferably as an ethnographically sensitive tool, thus has potential for sharpening our understanding of constructed commercial auditory spaces.

7 On the Town: Contesting Background Music

This section provides an analysis of the material side of background music auditory culture in situ: what is in fact audible and what is recognisable or meaningful. This section differs stylistically somewhat from the previous sections due to the experiential nature of the methods and the section's objective – to ethnographically convey the everyday experience of background music in city spaces. Our research data (listening diaries and interviews) is collated with aurally diverse listener-consumers. It shows that for people more sensitive to sensory stimuli than average, the volume and quality of background music influences, for example, choices such as which shops and restaurants to visit and selecting walking routes and times in the city. For the hard of hearing, exposing oneself to background music can muddle the communicative environment thoroughly or, if played at a relatively low volume, be fully filtered out by the sound processors in their neuroprosthetic hearing aid. (ACMEi 2022c; ACMEi 2022d.)

Variability of attention and distraction is a key area of interest in the study of the urban environment and mediated urban space. Sensory overload in the form of distraction is a characteristic long associated with urban life in general (Kytö 2020). Considerable fluctuation in attention levels is partly related to the conceptual distinction between active and passive listening (Kassabian 2013). This distinction has also been an essential element in examining the putative effects of background music. The soundscape of a shopping centre consists of sounds and listening situations specific to its functions, providing an acoustic frame for the (in)audibility of music. These include the queuing at the checkout, the whirring of the ventilation, the clinking of ice-cream cups, the weighing of fruit, the advice given to customers, the footsteps of security guards, the chatter of young people, and the shrieking of tired children. At times, it can be very challenging to hear or recognise any music, as the sound resonates in an acoustically opaque space (ACMEf/Kk).

In many of our fieldwork spaces, background music was played at a surprisingly low volume, so that musical elements were barely audible through the rest of the soundscape. Songs are often not heard from start to finish but as melodies here and there, in the time before the listener steps off the tram, gets in line at the checkout, chats with their tablemate, or changes equipment at the gym. The randomness of the encounters between music and listener-consumer is reinforced in the case of hallway music by the practice of placing spoken advertisements with jingles in the middle of the songs (ACMEi2019b).

One aspect in the overlapping of musical streams is probably characteristic of the North: thermal insulation between the inside and outside of commercial premises is very tight, at least during winter. The music seldom seeps outside, and environmental policy (together with cultural norms concerning acoustic territories) makes the use of outdoor loudspeakers sparse or temporarily specific to seasonal markets or sports events. Shopping centres are also places for getting warm during wintertime, so they get selected on walking routes in the urban landscape just to walk through. The material space of shopping centres means enclosed but roomy spaces designed for a variety of purposes: walkways, car parks, and cafés, spread out along the centre's corridors; department stores, where music from different departments mix randomly; specialised shops, restaurants, lifts, and thematic displays such as, for example, Christmas display windows with music playing in front. Hallway music ties together the nested and overlapping spaces, while the music of individual businesses separates them sonically.

Streaming music and the associated proliferation of playlists has created new music selection practices and built new relationships among actors. The music selection process has the potential for making background music a part of a small business's local identity or overall 'brand', and it can also be an expression of the personal tastes of employees. The choice of music can be guided by the business's needs by allowing staff to decide on the music to be

Figure 3 Old stereo including a CD and LP player buried under a desk at a skating store at Koskikeskus mall. The current playback system was an iMac tabletop computer ('Streaming is much more convenient'). The old equipment was kept "in case of special events with DJs". Picture: Meri Kytö.

played, particularly where staff are culturally similar to the target customers of the business (DeNora 2000: 137–138). Staff in restaurants and bars may take pride in the music they play to demonstrate their musical capital and create a sense of community in their workplace (ACMEf/Kk; ACMEf/Christmas). Sensory agency manifests itself through various tactics in the urban environment. Playlists can inform and advertise new music releases and remind about older favourites. This was a tactic of a gym instructor designing her new routines and choreographies we interviewed in Tampere. She rarely listened to the radio, but instead relied on background music in her favourite cafés and clubs for ideas and inspiration. For her, background music playlists had taken the role of recommender, traditionally a role for music journalists. (ACMEi 2020d.)

Background music practices in different environments allow for multiple levels of meaning-making and agency. In part, this music-related agency is part of the *spatial interpellation*, the recognition of ideology and its subjectification (see Althusser 1976: 40): the mall addresses its customers with music and the customer listening to the background music can assume the role of the customer. Failure of interpellation may lead to resistance, frustration, and irritation. Reverse interpellation occurs when technology fails, when there is no music in the hallways, or when there is a sudden change to calm, with the risk that visitors suspect the mall is closing down for the day, 'get confused, and leave' (ACMEi 2019c). The discussion of interpellation can be linked to the interaction between the background music and the listener and to how the music is expected to affect them. Hearing background music is ultimately about the urban environment in which the music 'publicly addresses' the subject. Instead of a stimulus, the subject takes the music as their own in the context in which it is played. In this event, the music, the subject's attention, memories, and the prevailing circumstances come together, bringing disparate and disjointed elements together into a larger whole (see also DeNora 2000: 42–3).

The listener-consumer is on the move; their experience of the background music is one of encountering overlapping sound sources, noticing musical elements that grow stronger and weaker, momentarily and randomly. Therefore, distraction, attention, movement, and intention can be used as key experiential elements and as methodological starting points when examining the perceptions of background music. While the initial intention of using background music may be to steer the customers' attention and actions in a desired direction, people frequently perceive music in more diverse and complex ways. The same music may feel calming or disturbing, depending on context and listener. For an employee, background music may appear as either an aid or a hindrance to concentration. Factors such as the listener's physiology, sensitivity, abilities, culture, identity, and musical preferences all affect how music is perceived in a given situation. Background music also does not play in a sonic vacuum but is embedded in the overall sonic environment. The experience of background music is formed in relation to other sounds from machines, crowds, and working.

7.1 Methodological Takeaways: Everyday Auditory Experience

To investigate the auditory experience of background music in the everyday urban environment, our research team tried out and further developed a selection of methods. There were two goals: to gain more detailed insights into the sonic reality of urban everyday life concerning background music listening and to question the strict division between the customer and the service employee. We collated research material through various coordinated observation methods, incorporating listening walks, music recognition apps, instant messaging, mapping, field recording, and sound diaries: a collage of methods familiar to sensory ethnography and soundscape studies that we ended up calling the 'AI-assisted Background Music Fieldwork Method'. While on the move, we were randomly inquired about our possible links with copyright organisations, meaning whether we were perhaps music license inspectors.

One data collection was conducted as a workshop of listening walks in Joensuu.[15] The collection was carried out by seven participants who walked a route of their own choice from the university campus to the city centre. The instructions were to visit spaces open to the public and to make observations of any music that might be playing. At the participants' disposal were Shazam and SoundHound music recognition apps, used as a support in identifying the songs heard. During the walks, it became clear that for an identifiable sample, music must be loud enough to be transmitted to the application. Moreover, Shazam did not always identify the correct recording or artist. This is presumably due to either the fact that unreleased live recordings are not stored in the database used by the application, or the difficulty the music recognition algorithm runs into when attempting to distinguish the required signal from the blurred soundscape. All quotations in the following section are copied from the fieldwork notes (ACMEf/Joensuu).

When there was music in an establishment, an employee was asked about the source and the choice of music ('Where does the music come from?' 'Who chooses the music?'). During three hours, the participants reported on fifty-three

---

[15] Joensuu is a university town close to the Russian border with a population of 77,000.

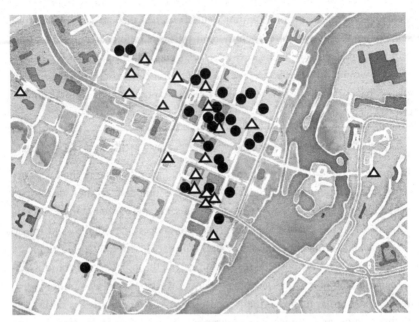

Figure 4 Downtown Joensuu. Dots show spaces with background music.
Triangles mark spaces without background music.

locations, thirty-two of which had background music playing. The participants
sent location data for each visited establishment to a WhatsApp group. The data
were used to draw up a map of the study sites (see Figure 4). The songs heard by
participants were compiled into a public playlist on Spotify.[16] Music sources
varied where background music was played:[17] laptops with integrated speakers,
portable cassette players, televisions, stereos or tablets connected to external
speakers, CD players, and portable radios. In larger spaces, speakers were embedded in the walls or ceilings. Fifteen sites played music from a radio station,
fourteen had music playing from a tailored service, and three used their own CDs.

The music played in Joensuu city centre shops was predominantly Anglo-
American popular music sung by men. Half of the recordings heard had been
released in the 2010s, and all of the music included vocals (there was no
instrumental music). English was the language sung in twenty-six songs,
Finnish in three, and Thai in one. Of the performers, nineteen were identifiable
as men, six as women, and five performances had both genders audible. Eleven

---

[16] https://open.spotify.com/playlist/0p0qhyhYMijoFq9BN5Vwwe?si=966ceebf0ce34199
[17] The establishments were five clothing stores, four restaurants or bars, four grocery stores, three
cafés, three barbershops, two gyms, two shopping centres or department stores, an office, a bank,
a games shop, a telecom operator's shop, a flea market, a bakery, a cosmetics shop, a sweet shop,
and an antiquarian bookshop.

singers were from North America, fifteen from Europe (including four from Finland), and three from Asia. Eight performances could be categorised as rock, heavy, or funk; thirteen as pop; and nine as soul, R&B, or hip-hop. In terms of quantity, the dominance of Anglo-American popular music in commercial spaces became evident with the exception of a Thai grocery store playing Thai pop music ('the choice of the lady of the house'), a case of vernacular cosmopolitanism of sorts (see Feld 2012). In twelve of the sites listened to, employees had no direct influence on the choice of music. In some sites, a background music service occasionally asked the staff for feedback on the playlists purchased from them. This was also the case in a shop that experimented with generative music mentioned earlier: the trial was interrupted after negative feedback from employees.

In her ethnographic study of IRCAM, the music anthropologist Georgina Born emphasised how the use of music technology is often presented as idealised, uncomplicated, and normative (Born 1995: 15). This conceptualisation is seldom solidly based in reality, which was evident in the case at hand. In two of the Joensuu study sites, faulty music equipment, radio reception, or the proximity of channels to the receiver were a headache ('We have a really awkward radio, always playing on some random channel'). Because the channel would not stay tuned, the solution was 'often to find any [channel] that stays on'. Everyday practices of using playback technology included learning, relearning, teaching others how to use the equipment, taking responsibility for its maintenance, or avoiding responsibility altogether. Many workers were unable or unwilling to say what the source of the music was: 'I don't know where it comes from, it comes from somewhere over there'; 'The tapes come from somewhere ready-made, we don't know, we don't even hear (the music) here' [makes a gesture with her hand from one ear in and out the other]. Nor do sales assistants and waiters 'have time' to pay attention to the matter while working. However, in general, the use of the music equipment was routine for many, with no music selection or adjustment of the equipment necessary ('I just turn a knob').

Our attention was drawn to the large number of places with no music and to the reasons for not playing music. Some sound systems were defunct and not repaired or replaced. Sometimes shopkeepers explained their mounted loudspeakers were unsuitably placed, causing their sound to be carried unnecessarily far from the shop premises. In some sites, playing music had been considered but deemed not important enough to warrant action ('sometimes we wonder if there should be something'). There were also reports of preferred sources of sound present in the premises, such as a television; or of different sound zones within the shop, reminiscent of the adult novelty shop case – for example, that music was only listened to in the back of the shop and not in the customer areas. Others felt that music was completely unnecessary ('there is none and there is no need'), while others justified the lack of music by the high cost of royalties ('those Gramex royalties are terrible, I never even thought of [having music here]').

7.2 Seasonal Disruption in Background Music Content: Christmas

The use of Christmas music to decorate the city is its own specific background music practice. As an exception, it disrupts the everyday sonic environment otherwise treated with indifference, avoidance, or disregard: the disruption draws attention to itself, although most people could not characterise what the 'usual' music in the environment sounded like. It is thus suitable for studying the experiential side of background music. In this section, we explore the experience of Christmassy background music in urban space and how it compares as a phenomenon with visual Christmas decoration practices (Kytö 2021). Visual decoration is the addition and repetition of elements that are characteristic of the festive season, culturally crystallised practices, and everyday aesthetics (Korolainen 2012: 11).

The religious and ideological nature of Christmas music is an interesting feature in background music content, otherwise designed to be neutral and unobtrusive. Our focus here is therefore in 'overheard' music, to which, despite its ephemeral nature, the listener can attach the same kind of meanings as to any musical performance, built on their cultural knowledge, personal memories, and preferences. We set out to find out whether or not they actually did, and what their experience was like.

Christmas music is seasonal – performed, listened to, and used as part of annual celebrations and customs. In Finland, the essence of this tradition is about shared musicking (Small 1998) in public spaces. Some of this live music is used as background music in shopping centres as a decorative element. Christmas background music in public and commercial spaces renews and produces musical traditions and also generates a lot of economic returns. These revenues accrue to both the music industry and the retail sector.

The festive season from November onwards with company and community Christmas parties (*pikkujoulu*, in Finnish) often includes musicking, participation in music through listening, and dancing, even if the music involved does not tend to be carol-oriented. The educational system has institutionalised Christmas music-making since the nineteenth century. Today, Christmas music is taught in schools, where the rehearsed pieces are performed at the end of the autumn term at the school's Christmas pageant. In churches, concert events quadruple in

December, frequently as community singing events. The public debate around Christmas background music is lively, with comments on the timing, choice, and repetition of music, volume, and temporary PA solutions.

In addition to the numerous international online radio stations that play only Christmas music, domestic alternatives include Nelonen Media's Radio Aalto,[18] which switches to Christmas music for the season, and the parish-run Jouluradio, which plays only Christmas music and is devoid of advertising. Jouluradio's Christmas music – spiritual and traditional Finnish Christmas music – is also popular with listeners. Streaming seasonal playlist services can be ordered as a ready-made service or compiled by entrepreneurs themselves. GT Musiikki-luvat provides businesses a checklist outlining current practices and professional recommendations, portraying playlist compiling as a job akin to decorating a shop and other Christmas decorations. They recommend a list of 250 to 300 songs to avoid repetition and staff boredom, as well as a bold mix of musical styles and song languages, calmer and more upbeat Christmas songs. Using playlists therefore requires more effort and planning than choosing a Christmas radio station, and the season brings its own aesthetic complications – 'Christmas music does not have to be all hopping elves or Christmas trees' (GT Musiikkiluvat 2021). Christmas background music not selected from radio or playlists is most likely a part of a commissioned background music product package, including playlists, voice-overs, and a sound system. These products follow the general pattern of increasing the recurrence of Christmas music the closer Christmas Eve gets: in November, around 10 per cent, rising to between 75 per cent and 100 per cent as Advent and different Christmas season opening events culminate in Christmas week. (ACMEi 2019b.)

Christmas music includes historical styles from several centuries. It is not genre-specific: identifying clear tonal or structural characteristics is difficult. The inherent religiosity and ideology of Christmas music is also an interesting feature in background music content, otherwise designed to be neutral and unobtrusive. All in all, the most distinct sonic feature of the Christmas period in the urban soundscape is a certain musical timbre, the *chime*. It adorns commercial spaces as well as religious places, elven lanterns, and church choirs and is a signifier of both 'the celebration of joy' and 'the peace of Christmas'. Musicologist Freya Jarman-Ivens calls this metallic sound 'musical tinsel' (Jarman-Ivens 2008: 115), while musicologist Todd Decker calls it a 'glistening timbre', which emerges from bell jingles, celestas, triangles, finger cymbals, and tubular bells and is present on almost every Christmas album since WWII (Decker 2020). Music historian Vesa Kurkela (1999) also draws attention

---

[18] From 2021 on, titled 'Me Naiset radio'; from 2023 on, titled 'Easy Hits'.

to the prominence of bright metallic sounds in Christmas entertainment music. Unlike Decker, he traces its origins to the nineteenth century, the golden age of Christmas music. The fashionable musical automatons and tavern pianos were phenomena of an industrialising and urbanising society. One could not avoid hearing them when walking through cities.

> The common features of the chiming (*kilinä*) environment were thus commercialism, amusement, urbanity and new technology, all important determinants of modern society in the 19th century. The sound of the sacred moment thus became the central expression of the most dynamic secular scene. (Kurkela 1999: 160)

Chiming sounds have a long history in religious music as a marker of a sacred moment. These sounds have come to signify what might be called, outside the ecclesiastical space, *the magic of Christmas*.

In this segment of the project, we chose a combination of autoethnography and crowdsourced data collection methods. The data, collected at the turn of 2019 and 2020, consists of listening observations (n=127) and of auto-ethnographic soundscape observations in the form of a listening diary (71 days). A sensory ethnographic method often used in soundscape research – and in this case, also an auto-ethnographic method – was writing a sound diary compiling observations of the everyday soundscape. From November to January, Meri Kytö made daily notes of all the music she heard in commercial or public spaces that she considered to be Christmas music. She also made observations in the form of more systematic recorded listening walks in shopping centres and Christmas markets and used a music recognition app to identify the songs she heard. Summaries of the recordings were published daily on a website.[19] Alongside the written field notes, reviewing the listening walk recordings proved useful for checking banalities and details overlooked in the situation. The sound diary as auto-ethnographic data provides a relatively private and individual understanding of the 'general' but is an excellent method for focusing on the small, everyday, and ordinary (see Uotinen 2010: 179, 186) changes in the soundscape during the Christmas season.

We also collected observations using the social media hashtag #joululaulubingo (#xmascarolbingo). We asked people to identify any Christmassy music they came across in public (with the use of Shazam or SoundHound app if possible) and to send us this information with a description of the place and situation.[20] The 129 observations from 49 #joululaulubingo participants are

---

[19] A compilation of all Christmassy music heard, reported, and available as recordings can be accessed on Spotify: https://open.spotify.com/playlist/6wj6lel3ultAvIBXIjFWTV? si=76a43b2131b944af.

[20] Using either a hashtag on Twitter, an email, or a direct social media message.

mainly reports of a few words or sentences in the form of instant messages, sent almost simultaneously in situ. We consider this a significant methodological advantage in the study of 'overheard' sounds: had the communication device not been at hand or a more complex reflection required, observations would very likely have gone unreported. Tapping a quick response to a simple collection invitation in the midst of other everyday activities was easy.

7.3 Analysis and Reflection on Seasonal Background Music

To answer questions about the experience of Christmas background music in urban space and its decorative seasonal nature, we have categorised the data under two experiential themes. These are related firstly to the stage of season: the chronological experiences of launching, high-season, and the anticipation of conclusion of the season; and secondly, the experience of positive, neutral, or negative contact: encountering and avoiding Christmassy music. All quotations in the section are from fieldwork notes (ACMEf/Christmas).

Exploring the idea of the annual cycle of decoration by applying it to soundscape and the Christmas season proved useful. Parallel to visual decoration, repertoire used as customary background music outside the Christmas season can be seen as 'fixed decoration', while the Christmas background music is 'festive decoration' (cf. Korolainen 2012: 46, 67). In the city, music is used to decorate many spaces and to build the atmosphere for Christmas tourism during the season in a ritualistic way. The atmosphere is built up on a smaller scale in, for example, swimming pools, taxis, or petrol stations, and on a larger scale with entire Christmas sections in department stores, where the music is also played at higher volume. Music-making associated with Christmas traditions is almost seamlessly integrated into functional music spaces, gym classes, and airports. Background music is introduced in places where it is not routinely present, using temporary loudspeaker systems in front of department store Christmas display windows and background music in Christmas markets. Like a glittering ornament, this sonic surprise element momentarily draws more attention to these expansions of commercial space.

Christmas marketing and the decorations associated with the festive season began to appear, especially in shopping centres, as early as October, becoming more abundant after Black Friday (the Friday after the fourth Thursday in November). Known in the United States as the opening day of the Christmas season for retailers, Black Friday has also become known in Finland as the discount day before the Christmas season. The earliest observations of recorded Christmassy music in the data are dated 8 November in Helsinki, in the restroom of a bar. From the end of November onwards, observations of the full start of the season were reported. Most of the reports and observations date back to the Christmas week, when presumably many of the participants in the data collection did their Christmas shopping. The full decoration with sounds and visual decorations corresponds to the full atmosphere: 'It was full steam ahead at the Pullman [bar] in Helsinki railway station just now! From "Winter Wonderland" to "Rudolph the Red-nosed Reindeer". Both as elevator music and sung.' Another participant noted that 'In Turku Walo [restaurant] today there were Christmas carols, Christmas decorations, mulled wine, and the staff had ironic Christmas sweaters ;-)', and that 'The background music in the [railway] station's lobby has also been updated to include the rattling of sleigh bells and other Christmassy sounds'. Meanwhile, many also consistently reported that they had not ('still not') heard any Christmas music while walking around the city. This suggests that the experience of Christmas background music is not the same to everyone.

Based on the data, the aural Christmas season begins even earlier than the noted observation from a public restroom, with subtle and contagious musical incidents that are more difficult to categorise as background music. On the first day of November, a participant reported that in a staff restaurant 'someone sat at an untuned piano and fumbled a verse of the carol "Silent Night"'. From November onwards, reports of schoolchildren and nursery school children singing at home increased. Children were practising for the upcoming Christmas performances, carrying the songs home from nursery and school by humming and recalling melodies. Live Christmas music increased at events and in situations where background music was otherwise provided by recordings. Restaurants organised Christmas karaoke. Gyms had spinning classes to Christmas background music and 'Merry Christmas Carol' live performances. Choirs performed at Helsinki Airport, dressed up as elves, accompanied by Father Christmas characters. As the data collection progressed, the original plan to limit the focus to recordings and to public and commercial spaces began to look like a forced limitation in light of the ubiquitous sonic phenomenon as a whole.

According to the local Christian calendar, the Christmas holidays end on 6 January, Epiphany. The commercial Christmas season wanes, with varying degrees of intensity, after Christmas Day, in the early weeks of January. The last observation of Christmas background music is dated 4 January, in front of the Christmas display window of a department store. The end of the background music season is therefore not entirely in line with the commercial seasonal calendar. Without a sound diary, it is more difficult to report hearing the last song of the season. For this understandable reason, reports of hearing Christmas carols after Christmas Eve dried up. According to the project's own sound diary, the fading of Christmas elements in the soundscape happened quickly: the chiming faded. After St John's Day, 27 December, the sound diary mentions no Christmas background music, with the exception of the aforementioned Sokos Christmas display window front.

The familiarity and repetitiveness of the melodies means tunes and lyrics can get stuck in people's minds. They take up more space in the mind than the time of actually hearing the song, which can be just a few seconds. As an experiential phenomenon, musical contagion is similar to the notion of co-subjectivity. DeNora (2000: 149–50) uses the term to refer to the ways in which people can experience and present similar feelings and behaviours in relation to external parameters (such as those provided by music). This kind of co-subjectivity is distinct from the notion of intersubjectivity, which presupposes dialogue, reflexivity, and the co-production of meanings between experiencers. Co-subjectivity is the result of the individual's own reflexive relationship with the environment and its materiality. Often inadvertently produced for the self, humming and whistling have less of an intersubjective dimension and a pronounced level of co-subjectivity.

The ephemeral and transient nature of music listening caused difficulties in reporting. Reports sometimes indicated Christmas music had been heard but that over the course of the day, the memory of what exactly it had been had faded. The momentariness of the situations and their presumed insignificance also caused hesitation regarding sending notifications, although by nature they were technically easy mobile instant messaging. In such observations, Christmas music appeared as a small element in the soundscape – implying not yet a beginning of the season but an anticipation of it.

The repetitiveness of Christmas background music is ironically highlighted in the game of *not* hearing Wham!'s 'Last Christmas' before Christmas Eve. Upon encountering the song somewhere one loses the game and shall report this on social media using the tag #whamageddon. Licensed restaurants and some events have adapted the game for their business interests by advertising they will not be playing the song. The Finnish counterpart in 2019 was #loirigeddon, where the aim was not to hear Vesa-Matti Loiri singing 'Sydämeeni joulun teen'. The game predicted the most repetitive and ubiquitous Finnish Christmas song.[21]

---

[21] According to Gramex (2020), 'Last Christmas' was the most played Christmas song on commercial radio in Finland in 2019 (902 radio plays, six mentions in the data). The second most played song was Mariah Carey's 'All I Want for Christmas Is You' (781 radio plays, four mentions in the data). The third overall (and first domestic) song on the list was Loiri's 'Sydämeeni joulun teen' (587 radio plays). Despite the high number of radio plays, no one in the ACMEf/Christmas data had heard Loiri in 2019.

An important point to note when analysing the ACMEf/Christmas data is that none of the respondents reported working in the service sector. In another of our surveys (ACMEs/PAM 2021), service sector employees were asked about the seasons of background music. Christmas music was mentioned as 'good Christmas music' that increases enjoyment and is a 'nice change'. In line with the stage-of-season-related comments from social media participants, a shop assistant wrote: 'In October, a small-scale battle starts, when myself and a few others would be ready to switch to Christmas music, but others think it's still too early' (ACMEs/PAM 2021d). However, working amidst Christmas music was also perceived by some as a burden lasting for an unreasonably long time. The annoyance was often caused by a too-short playlist, resulting in repetition. This caused one respondent to not want to listen to Christmas music at home at all, 'or any music in general' (ACMEs/PAM 2021e). Excessive decoration with music may lead to an experience of genuine disgust and affect everyday music practices in general.

The Christmas music heard in commercial spaces mixes traditional music with the logic of financial gain and is comparable to the commodification and technologisation of ambience (see Thibaud 2020). Background music products are increasingly being developed towards multisensoriality. For example, at Christmas 2019, the Stockmann department store in Tampere had added a fir-tree scenting system in their entrance corridor. These expanding design trends are also convergent and can be seen as processes where decorating transforms towards advertising. Theorising the transformation of sensory environments in cities, Jean-Paul Thibaud (2020) wants us to look past these processes and rather pay attention to *ambient sensitivity*, highlighting the diffuse, affective, and pervasive nature of any sensory experience. Thibaud stresses the power of such sensitivity to strengthen and transform our relations with the world. Like many theorists of sensory experience, Thibaud wants to increase the agency of the subject as owner of and knowledgeable about their sensory experiences. This has been our aim as well: we have sought to show how the everyday experience of overhearing background music is more varied and nuanced than is suggested by those who sell background music products.

8 Discussion

We have aimed to incite interest in and discussion on the 'music that nobody listens to' – the background music cultures that reveal both general and locally specific characteristics. This discussion concerns planning of urban areas, aesthetic design of acoustic spaces, the discourse of individual and collective well-being with music, and defining the urban sonic identity. It benefits from insight into the current trends of background music such as centralised music selection, digitalisation, the shift from background music to foreground music, and focusing on diverse target audiences. Discussion on background music extends to professional identities, aural diversity, musical breathing space, the transforming media environment (from hardware to software, from carriers to streams, from pseudo-scientific selection to algorithmic automation), and media content. The ample use of music experienced as familiar is key in understanding the long-lived critical discussions on the phenomenon of background music – generally understood as industry-led, behavioural, and global.

Issues on background music content such as selected or banned songs or artists raise questions about international industry standards, ideologies, and cultural values that may or may not be applicable in all cultural contexts. Questions of morality, ethics, and legislation need to be further critically assessed when background music programming processes are combined with analysis of data from other digital sources such as facial recognition for in situ music selection.

Although background music company personnel underline their agencies and competences in selecting music compilations for their clients, music is currently also identified and ordered by software algorithms on the basis of computational parameters, that is, 'listened to' by machines. This raises new questions about agency, listenership, and the supposed effects of background music. The parameters used in music selection processes are complex and extracted from the logic of capitalist accumulation (Zuboff 2015). Anthropologist and software researcher Adrian Mackenzie notes (2006: 5) that software has a secondary agency: it is not self-aware but is nevertheless capable of making relatively complex and autonomous decisions according to instructions it receives (see also Kitchin & Dodge 2011: 5). This is an agency handed over to the music selection algorithms, based on the cooperation between the user and the programme. In our view, the parameter-oriented machine listening is audible in some playlists studied during this project.

This frame of transferred agency opens up yet another perspective on the purpose and impact of music: what we understand the impact of music to be, who we expect music to affect, and how the music industry responds to this need or, alternatively, creates and sustains these needs. The discussion can be extended beyond the public sphere to listening in the private sphere and, somewhat surprisingly, to how music is assumed to affect living organisms other than human beings. The Spotify streaming service offers playlists of Western world mood music for pets and houseplants ('Music for Cats', 'Calming Sounds for Dogs'; 'Music for Plants'). Cats, dogs, and plants might or might not enjoy mood music, but as a strategy, keeping music streaming even when humans leave the house is a novel way to accumulate playback figures. Leaving the radio or TV on to keep pets company is an older urban habit, but here the argument for mood music is – again – presented as an affective need, in this setting for non-humans. The agency handed over to background music and the music's supposed effects meet in a new way in the context of a digital revenue model. For the provider of the music, the question of building a new consumer segment is central, while the motives of the end user are subject to speculation. What is interesting from a research point of view, however, is that this anthropocentric view is increasingly believed to extend the impact of background music beyond the human experience.

Musically speaking, the dishearkened listener-consumer is catered to with a plethora of musical expressions. Although describing background music through genres is almost impossible (as noted earlier in Figure 1), it is nevertheless feasible to make some musical observations from the sonic material gathered during our project. Recurrent features in the material include a certain kind of flatness or uniformity in dynamics, tempo, and expression, combined with an instrumentation favourable to compression. Rather than inspecting each tune individually, its functionality as background music can be deduced from the musical similarity it has with the preceding tune and the one that follows it. In other words, it is dependent on the temporal proximity of other similar songs.

The concept of 'functional music literacy' we coined in the Introduction involves awareness and skills that are necessary tools for those interested in understanding music and sound in its social, cultural, and political contexts. The understanding we have set our sights on building combines historical awareness with the analysis of agencies (both human and non-human), spatial factors, and cultural conventions of the present.

The points we presented earlier as context-specific to Finland can be extrapolated to assist in planning culture-sensitive background music research as a sort of checklist – suggestions, methodological observations, and aspects for future research and understanding of urban sonic environments. We now remould them as questions for consideration when drafting a research plan for a background music culture.

(1) Infrastructural:

- What developments in shopping and service consumption are characteristic to this culture?
- How are shopping areas in and outside cities organised spatially, socially, and sonically?
- Which public listening/broadcasting/sonic marketing practices are specific and/or historically significant to the culture in question (loudspeaker

cars, mobile listening, loudspeaker broadcasts, sonic practices related to CCTV, etc.)?

• What are the central developments concerning available technology, and how have they enabled music to be played/broadcast/reproduced?

(2) Societal and Economic:

• Which laws, regulations, and social norms concern the use and role of music and the media?

• Are there significant differences between insiders and outsiders (those who visit) in the culture when it comes to norms and everyday practices? For instance, is it advisable, appropriate, or even safe for tourists, women, persons with disabilities, or religious or sexual minorities to spend time in city spaces, and how does sound enter into the equation?

• How much (if any) of the music-makers' income derives from background music use? What are the positions and networks that exist for copyright organisations and unions for composers and musicians in the society?

• Do service sector employees have agency – collaborative or individual – in the sonic design of their work environment?

(3) Cultural:

• What musical characteristics (genres, artists, cultural/historical associations, language matters, etc.) are especially relevant to consumption and urban life in the culture at hand?

• Are there special points of contact between the service culture and the sonic culture (e.g. the role of verbal vs. nonverbal communication in service encounters, the noise level viewed appropriate for customer comfort, etc.)?

• How and why have certain sonic practices in public spaces been established? What normative thinking exists concerning noise in urban environments? Is mundane noise, such as annunciators or traffic sounds (honking, speeding, sirens), regulated? What are the attitudes towards unsought music in various contexts?

• What kinds of agency is background music given and assumed to have? How are these assumptions and transfers of agency manifested?

• In which ways is the diversity of hearing taken into consideration in urban spaces?

Research should not be restricted solely to sound or sonic environments, but encompass environments designed to stimulate the whole sensorium. Walking methods (sound walks, listening walks, sensory walks) have been important elements in soundscape research and sensory studies for half a century, and they are under continuous development (see e.g. Drever 2020; Järviluoma & Murray 2023; Smolicki 2023). Commercial city spaces often contain zones of fluctuating reality (e.g. embarrassing product zones, or experience industry services such as escape rooms, day spas, etc.). These zones indicate a need for *a holistic approach*: they may be soundproof in the physical sense, but experientially, they are not isolated. Paying attention to the zoned essence of the public and semi-public urban spaces is very much a holistic endeavour. Not every transition from one zone to another is as distinct as, for example, the tricky step from street space to sex shop premises, but nearly all of them have consequences for the listener-consumer's and the employees' experiences. Thus, the transitions are most often thought out by someone planning the soundscape, and as such, they merit culturally sensitive scrutiny.

Research Material

ACMESOCS Project Materials

Fieldwork notes of the project:

ACMEf/Joensuu: Joensuu city centre listening walks and mapping, 26 Oct 2019. Participants: Salli Anttonen, Kaarina Kilpiö, Meri Kytö, Janette Leino, Henna-Riikka Peltola, Heikki Uimonen, and Juhana Venäläinen.

ACMEf/Kk: Koskikeskus mall field observations, 2–4 Mar 2020, Meri Kytö and Heikki Uimonen.

ACMEf/Christmas: Heard Christmas music during 1 Nov 2019–10 Jan 2020, crowdsourced field observations (fifty-four Facebook entries, twenty-seven Messenger messages, nineteen WhatsApp messages, fourteen Twitter posts), auto-ethnographic sound diaries (seventy-one days, Meri Kytö), three recorded listening walks.

ACMEf/Sex: Adult retail stores field material (Lahti field diaries, 2022, Kaarina Kilpiö).

ACMEf/Ad: Aurally diverse listener-consumers' sound diaries, three participants, 2022–3.

Interviews conducted by project researchers (total: background music agency personnel (20), shopping centre directors (2), service sector personnel (10), radio programme directors (2), copyright organisation representatives (4), former sales secretaries and representatives in Finnish background music companies (6, conducted in 2005–6), aurally diverse listener-consumers (4), sex shop sales assistants/managers (3), gym instructor (1)).

- ACMEi 2019a: head of audio branding, Bauer Media
- ACMEi 2019b: Mall Voice (group interview)
- ACMEi 2019c: shopping centre director
- ACMEi 2020a: DjOnline (group interview)
- ACMEi 2020b: Mood Media (group interview)
- ACMEi 2020c: Audience First (group interview)
- ACMEi 2020d: gym instructor
- ACMEi 2021a: head of radio and audio, Yleisradio
- ACMEi 2021b: content director, Radio Nova
- ACMEi 2021c: chief digital officer, Teosto
- ACMEi 2021d: Viihdeväylä (online group interview)

- ACMEi 2022a: head of audio branding, Bauer Media
- ACMEi 2022b: sex shop manager, born 1987
- ACMEi 2022c: aurally diverse interviewee (sensoneurally challenged listener)
- ACMEi 2022d: aurally diverse interviewee (hard-of-hearing hearing aid user)

Photographs by ACMESOCS project
ACMEp 2020: Photograph of background system 8-hour-long cassette, Audience First premises, photographer Heikki Uimonen.

Surveys conducted by the ACMESOCS project
ACMEs/Kk 2020: Employee survey conducted with shopkeepers, waiters, and cleaning personnel (n=70) in 2020 at the Koskikeskus mall, Tampere
- ●ACMEs/Kk 2020a: respondent 17, female, born 1956, seamstress
- ●ACMEs/Kk 2020b: respondent 2, female, born 1975, retail sector
ACMEs/PAM2021: Service sector personnel online survey (n=747) conducted in 2021 in collaboration with the Finnish service workers' union PAM. Data available at https://etsin.fairdata.fi/dataset/ef83edcd-1b90-4616-aedf-1d04ede8e746.
- ACMEs/PAM 2021a: respondent 645, female, born 1967, grocery retail
- ACMEs/PAM 2021b: respondent 85, female, born 1965, commercial, real estate
- ACMEs/PAM 2021c: respondent 99, female, born 1974, retail sector
- ACMEs/PAM 2021d: respondent 628, female, born 1984, hotel sector
- ACMEs/PAM 2021e: respondent 271, male, born 1966, retail sector

Additional Research Material

Alko (2022). 5-4-3-2-1-0: Alkon historia. *Alko*. www.alko.fi/alko-oy/yritys/5-4-3-2-1-0#keskiolut%20kauppoihin (Accessed 14 Dec 2022).

City of Helsinki (1970). *Tutkimusselostus N:o 8-70: Työpaikkamusiikin vaikutus*. Helsingin kaupunginhallituksen järjestelytoimisto.

Gramex (2020). *Sydämeeni joulun teen radioiden soitetuin kotimainen joululaulu*. www.gramex.fi/sydameeni-joulun-teen-radioiden-soitetuin-kotimainen/3254/ (Accessed 12 Jan 2023).

GT Musiikkiluvat (2021). *Jouluinen musiikki yrityksissä: näin erotut joukosta ja rakennat juhlatunnelmaa musiikilla*. www.musiikkiluvat.fi/kuulokanavalla/nain-yritys-erottautuu-joulumusiikilla/ (Accessed 11 Jan 2023).

GT Musiikkiluvat (2022). *About Us*. www.musiikkiluvat.fi/en/about-us/ (Accessed 11 Jan 2023).

Helsingin Sanomat (1961). Taustamusiikkia työpaikoille. 12 Oct.

Helsingin Sanomat (1981). Yleisöltä [opinion piece]. 16 Jan.

Hietanoro, J. (2006). Interview of a former sales representative at *Musiikki Fazer* background music services, later *M&M Viihdepalvelu*. Interviewer Kaarina Kilpiö.

Lindén, K. (2006). Interview of a former Finnestrad sales director. Interviewer Kaarina Kilpiö.

Miettinen, J. (2006). Interview of a former background music salesman at *Musiikki Fazer*. Interviewer Kaarina Kilpiö.

The New Yorker (2006). The soundtrack of your life. www.newyorker.com/magazine/2006/04/10/the-soundtrack-of-your-life (Accessed 14 Dec 2022).

Paukku, E. (2006). Interview of a former background music sales director. Interviewer Kaarina Kilpiö.

Sound Agency (2014). *Sound agency*. www.slideshare.net/thesoundagency/credentials-case-studies-the-sound-agency (Accessed 25 Jan 2023).

Uusi Suomi (1961). Muzag-musiikkia Suomeenkin. 13 Oct.

References

Literature

Ala-Fossi, M. (2005). *Saleable compromises: Quality cultures in Finnish and US commercial radio*. Tampere: Tampere University Press.

Althusser, L. (1976). Idéologie et appareils idéologiques d'État. In *Positions (1964–1975)*. Paris: Les Éditions sociales, pp. 67–125.

Amphoux, P. (1993). *L'identité sonore des villes Européennes: guide méthodologique à l'usage des gestionnaires de la ville, des techniciens du son et des chercheurs en sciences sociales*. Grenoble: Cresson.

Anderson, B. (2020). *Kuvitellut yhteisöt: Nationalismin alkuperän ja leviämisen tarkastelua* [Imagined communities: Reflections on the origin and spread of nationalism]. Trans. Joel Kuortti. Tampere: Vastapaino.

Anderson, P. A. (2015). Neo-Muzak and the business of mood. *Critical Inquiry* 41(4), 811–40. https://doi.org/10.1086/681787.

Andersson, P. K. (2016). *Changing the servicescape: The influence of music, self-disclosure and eye gaze on service encounter experience and approach-avoidance behavior*. [Doctoral thesis]. Karlstad University, Faculty of Arts and Social Sciences, Department of Social and Psychological Studies. www.diva-portal.org/smash/get/diva2:1033521/FULLTEXT01.pdf.

Baumgarten, L. (2012). *Elevator going down: The story of Muzak*. Red Bull Music Academy Daily. https://daily.redbullmusicacademy.com/2012/09/history-of-muzak (Accessed 14 Dec 2022).

Bergholm, T. (2001). Suomen autoistumisen yhteiskuntahistoriaa. In K. Toiskallio, ed., *Viettelyksen vaunu: Autoilukulttuurin muutos Suomessa*. Helsinki: SKS, pp. 65–92.

Blacking, J. (1973). *How musical is man?* Seattle: University of Washington Press.

Born, G. (1995). *Rationalizing culture: IRCAM, Boulez, and the institutionalization of the musical avant-garde*. Berkeley: University of California Press.

Born, G. (2013). *Music, sound and space: Transformations of public and private experience*. Cambridge: Cambridge University Press. https://doi.org/10.1017/CBO9780511675850.

Boschi, E., Kassabian, A. & Quiñones, M.G. (2013). Introduction. In M. García Quiñones, A. Kassabian, & E. Boschi, eds., *Ubiquitous musics: The everyday sounds that we don't always notice*. Farnham: Ashgate, pp. 1–12.

Brun, L. (2021). *Radion kuuntelu Suomessa 2021*. Finnpanel.

Bull, M. (2013). Remaking the urban: The audiovisual aesthetics of iPod use. In J. Richardson, C. Gorbman, & C. Vernallis, eds., *The Oxford handbook of new audiovisual aesthetics*. Oxford: Oxford University Press, pp. 628–44.

Carbaugh, D., Berry, M., & Nurmikari-Berry, M. (2006). Coding personhood through cultural terms and practices: Silence and quietude as a Finnish 'natural way of being'. *Journal of Language and Social Psychology* 25(3), 203–20. https://doi.org/10.1177/0261927X06289422.

Carlén, S. (2018). *Musik i butik: En studie av hur musik påverkar handelsanställdas arbetsmiljö*. Handelsanställdas förbund Handels rapporter 5.

Cohen, L. (2003). *A consumers' republic: The politics of mass consumption in postwar America*. New York: Vintage Books.

Dahl, D. W., Manchanda, R. V., & Argo, J. J. (2001). Embarrassment in consumer purchase, the roles of social presence and purchase familiarity. *Journal of Consumer Research* 28(3), 473–81. https://doi.org/10.1086/323734.

Davis, M. S. (1983). *Smut: Erotic reality / obscene ideology*. Chicago: University of Chicago Press. https://doi.org/10.7208/chicago/9780226162461.001.0001.

Decker, T. (2020). Carols and music since 1900. In T. Larsen, ed., *The Oxford handbook of Christmas*. London: Oxford University Press, pp. 330–45. https://doi.org/10.1093/oxfordhb/9780198831464.013.28.

de Certeau, M. (2013). *Arkipäivän kekseliäisyys 1: Tekemisen tavat*. Trans. Tapani Kilpeläinen. Tampere: niin & näin.

DeNora, T. (2000). *Music in everyday life*. Cambridge: Cambridge University Press. https://doi.org/10.1017/CBO9780511675850.

Dibben, N., & Haake, A. B. (2013). Music and the construction of space in office-based work settings. In G. Born, ed., *Music, sound and space: Transformations of public and private experience*. Cambridge: Cambridge University Press, pp. 151–68.

Drever, J. L. (2020). Listening as methodological tool: Sounding soundwalking methods. In M. Bull and M. Cobussen, eds., *The Bloomsbury handbook of sonic methodologies*. London: Bloomsbury Academic, pp. 599–613.

EU (2021). Data protection under GDPR. *Your Europe: An official website of the European Union*. https://europa.eu/youreurope/business/dealing-with-custom ers/data-protection/data-protection-gdpr/index_en.htm (Accessed 14 Jan. 2022).

Feld, S. (1996). Waterfalls of song. An acoustemology of place in resounding in Bosawi, Papua New Guinea. In S. Feld & K. H. Basso, eds., *Senses of place*. Santa Fe, NM: School of American Research Press, pp. 91–135.

Feld, S. (2012). *Jazz cosmopolitanism in Accra: Five musical years in Ghana*. Durham, NC: Duke University Press.

Finlex (1993/2017). *Act on Yleisradio Oy.* www.finlex.fi/en/laki/kaannokset/ 1993/en19931380 (Accessed 25 Jan. 2023).

Frith, S. (1998). *Performing rites: On the value of popular music.* Cambridge, MA: Harvard University Press.

Gramex (2019). *Gramexin avoimuusraportti vuodelta 2019.* www.gramex.fi/ wp-content/uploads/2018/10/Avoimuusraportti-yhdistyksen-kokouksen-käsittelyyn-2.pdf (Accessed 14 Dec. 2022).

Haapala, P., & Peltola, J. (2018). Elinkeinorakenne 1750–2000. In P. Haapala, ed., *Suomen rakennehistoria: Näkökulmia muutokseen ja jatkuvuuteen (1400–2000).* Tampere: Vastapaino, pp. 170–209.

Hankonen, J. (1994). *Lähiöt ja tehokkuuden yhteiskunta.* Tampere University of Technology, Architecture. Tampere: Gaudeamus.

Heinonen, V., & Pantzar, M. (2002). Little America: The modernization of the Finnish consumer society in the 1950s and 1960s. In M. Kipping and N. Tiratsoo, eds., *Americanisation in 20th century Europe: Business, culture, politics.* Volume 2. Lille: Centre de Recherche sur l'Histoire de l'Europe du Nord-Ouest, Université Charles de Gaulle, pp. 41–59.

Hesmondhalgh, D. (2002). Popular music audiences and everyday life. In D. Hesmondhalgh & K. Negus, eds., *Popular music studies.* London: Arnold, pp. 117–30.

Hesmondhalgh, D. (2019). *The cultural industries.* 4th ed. Los Angeles: Sage.

Hopkins, J. (1994). Orchestrating an indoor city: Ambient noise inside a mega-mall. *Environment and Behaviour* 26(6), 785—812. https://doi.org/ 10.1177/0013916594266004.

Horkheimer, M., & Adorno, T. W. (2008). *Valistuksen dialektiikka: Filosofisia sirpaleita.* Tampere: Vastapaino.

Hujanen, T. (2001). Ääniradio. In K. Nordenstreng and O. A. Wiio, eds., *Suomen mediamaisema.* Helsinki: WSOY, pp. 93–113.

Hukari, V. (2021). *Jäätynyt konflikti: Vähittäiskaupan keskittynyt kilpailutilanne Suomessa.* Licenciate thesis, University of Vaasa/Economics and Business Administration. https://urn.fi/URN:NBN:fi-fe202101151926

Husch, J. A. (1984). *Music of the workplace: A study of Muzak culture.* PhD thesis, University of Massachusetts.

ICRT (2022). *Information Centre of Road Transport: Vehicles in traffic use.* https://www.aut.fi/en/statistics/vehicle_fleet/vehicles_in_traffic_use (Accessed 7 Dec. 2022).

Jacob, C., Guéguen, N., Boulbry, G., & Sami, S. (2009). 'Love is in the air': Congruence between background music and goods in a florist. *The International Review of Retail, Distribution and Consumer Research* 19(1), 75–9. https://doi.org/10.1080/09593960902781334.

Jarman-Ivens, F. (2008). The musical underbelly of Christmas. In S. Whiteley, ed., *Christmas, ideology and popular culture*. Edinburgh: Edinburgh University Press, pp. 113–34.

Järviluoma, H., & Murray, L., eds. (2023). *Sensory transformations: Environments, technologies, sensobiographies*. New York: Routledge.

Johnson, B., & Cloonan, M. (2009). *Dark side of the tune: Popular music and violence*. Ashgate: Burlington.

Kang, J., & Yi, F. (2019). Effect of background and foreground music on satisfaction, behavior, and emotional responses in public spaces of shopping malls. *Applied Acoustics* 145 (February), 408–19.

Karlsen, S. (2019). Agency. *The SAGE international encyclopedia of music and culture*. Ed. J. Sturman. Sage Publications.

Kassabian, A. (2001). *Hearing film: Tracking identifications in contemporary Hollywood film music*. New York: Routledge.

Kassabian, A. (2006 [1999]). Popular. In B. Horner and T. Swiss, eds., *Key terms in popular music and culture*. Malden: Blackwell, pp. 113–23.

Kassabian, A. (2013). *Ubiquitous listening: Affect, attention, and distributed subjectivity*. Berkeley: University of California Press. https://doi.org/ 10.1525/california/9780520275157.001.0001.

Kauhanen, A., & Nevavuo, J. (2021). *Neuvottelujärjestelmät: Tutkimustuloksia ja maiden välisiä vertailuja*. ETLA Report No. 110. Helsinki: The Research Institute of the Finnish Economy (ETLA). https://pub.etla.fi/ETLA-Raportit-Reports-110.pdf (Accessed 21 Dec. 2022).

Kemppainen, P. (2001). *Radion murros: Julkisradioiden suuri kanavauudistus Norjassa, Ruotsissa ja Suomessa*. Helsinki: University of Helsinki.

Kilpiö, K. (2001). Kulkevat kauppiaat vuosisadan takaisissa suomalaisissa äänimuistoissa. *Etnomusikologian vuosikirja* 13, 62–74. https://doi.org/ 10.23985/evk.101120.

Kilpiö, K. (2005). *Kulutuksen sävel: Suomalaisen mainoselokuvan musiikki 1950-luvulta 1970-luvulle*. Helsinki: Like.

Kilpiö, K. (2011). Alitajunnan ohjailemisesta profiloitumiseen: taustamusiikkituotteiden muutoksia 1900-luvun Suomessa. *Musiikin suunta* 33(2), 11–17.

Kilpiö, K. (2013). From background to foreground: Music products for production and consumption spaces. In V. Heinonen and M. Peltonen, eds., *Finnish consumption: An emerging consumer society between east and west*. Helsinki: The Finnish Literature Society, pp. 230–51.

Kilpiö, K. (2016). Kuuntelevat kuluttajat 1950–1980-lukujen Suomessa: Myynninedistämismusiikin ammattilaiset ja heidän 'yleisönsä'. In H. Järviluoma and U. Piela, eds., *Äänimaisemissa*. Helsinki: The Finnish Literature Society, pp. 222–42.

Kilpiö, K. (2023). Äänellinen vyöhykkeistäminen kuluttajatarjouman rakentamisessa: etnografinen tutkimus lahtelaisten seksikauppojen ääniympäristöistä. *Kulttuurintutkimus* 40(3), 24–44. https://journal.fi/kulttuurintutkimus/article/view/122630.

Kilpiö, K., Kurkela, V., & Uimonen, H. (2015). *Koko kansan kasetti: C-kasetin käyttö ja kuuntelu Suomessa*. Suomalaisen Kirjallisuuden Seuran toimituksia 1413.

Kilpiö, K., & Kytö, M. (2021). Hyvinvointi taustamusiikin kokemuksissa: Palvelualalla toimivien näkemykset työskentelystä musiikin kanssa. *Musiikki* 51(4), 19–49. https://doi.org/10.51816/musiikki.113247.

Kitchin, R., & Dodge, M. (2011). *Code/Space: Software and everyday life*. Cambridge, MA: MIT Press.

Knöferle, K. M., Spangenberg, E. R., Herrmann, A., & Landwehr, J. R. (2011). It is all in the mix: The interactive effect of music tempo and mode on in-store sales. *Marketing Letters* 23(1), 1–13.

Kokko, H. (2016). Puhelinlangat laulaa: Puhelinpalveluiden odotusmusiikki käyttömusiikkina. MA thesis. University of Tampere. https://urn.fi/URN:NBN:fi:uta-201605101541.

Komulainen, A. (2018). *Valloittavat osuuskaupat: Päivittäistavarakaupan keskittyminen Suomessa 1879–1938*. PhD thesis, University of Helsinki. http://urn.fi/URN:ISBN:978-952-94-1077-4.

Kontukoski, M., & Uimonen, H. (2019). Tila, tunne ja musiikki: Kauppakeskuksen ääniympäristön laadullinen tarkastelu. *Yhdyskuntasuunnittelu* 57(2), 10–25. https://doi.org/10.33357/ys.83675.

Korolainen, K. (2012). *Koristelun kuvailu: Kategorisoinnin analyysi*. Publications of the University of Eastern Finland. Dissertations in Education, Humanities, and Theology 32. Joensuu: University of Eastern Finland. http://urn.fi/URN:ISBN:978-952-61-0855-1.

Krajina, Z., & Stevenson, D. (2020). General introduction. In Z. Krajina and D. Stevenson, eds., *The Routledge companion to urban media and communication*. London: Routledge, pp. 1–6.

Kurkela, V. (1999/2019). 1800-luvun sointikuva ja populaarimusiikki: Lähtökohtia varhaisen populaarimusiikin soinnin tutkimiseen. *Etnomusikologian vuosikirja* 31, 143–66. https://doi.org/10.23985/evk.86179.

Kurkela, V., Lahti, M., Uimonen, H., & Heikkinen, O. (2009). Medioitua vai medioimatonta? *Musiikin suunta* 31(3), 3–5.

Kurkela, V., & Uimonen, H. (2009). Demonopolizing Finland: The changing contents of Finnish commercial and public radios, 1980–2005. *Radio Journal* 7(2), 135–54.

Kytö, M. (2013). *Kotiin kuuluvaa: yksityisen ja yhteisen kaupunkiäänitilan risteymät.* Dissertations in Education, Humanities, and Theology 45. Joensuu: Itä-Suomen yliopisto.

Kytö, M. (2016). Asumisen rajat: yksityinen äänimaisema naapurisuhteita käsittelevissä nettikeskusteluissa. In H. Järviluoma and U. Piela, eds., *Äänimaisemissa.* Helsinki: The Finnish Literature Society, pp. 53–70.

Kytö, M. (2020). The senses and the city: Attention, distraction and media technology in urban environments. In Z. Krajina and D. Stevenson, eds., *The Routledge companion to urban media and communication.* London: Routledge, pp. 371–8. https://doi.org/10.4324/9781315211633-39/.

Kytö, M. (2021). Sesonkiäänimaisema kaupungissa: jouluinen taustamusiikki kalendaarisena koristeluna. *Elore* 28(2), 68–88. https://doi.org/10.30666/elore.110825.

Lacey, K. (2013). *Listening publics: The politics and listening in the media age.* Cambridge: Polity Press.

Lanza, J. (1995). *Elevator music: A surreal history of Muzak, easy-listening and other moodsong.* London: Quartet Books.

Lanza, J. (2013). Foreground flatland. In J. Richardson, C. Gorbman, & C. Vernallis, eds., *The Oxford handbook of new audiovisual aesthetics.* Oxford: Oxford University Press, pp. 622–7.

Mackenzie, A. (2006). *Cutting code: Software and sociality.* New York: Peter Lang.

Mäkelä, J. (2017). Oikeuden soitto: Lainsäädäntö ja musiikkikulttuuri Suomessa 1968–1999. *Musiikin suunta* 39(3). http://musiikinsuunta.fi/2017/03/oikeuden-soitto/

Malina, D., & Schmidt, R. A. (1997). It's business doing pleasure with you: Sh! A women's sex shop case. *Marketing Intelligence & Planning* 15(6–7), 352–60. https://doi.org/10.1108/02634509710367926.

Milliman, R. E. (1982). Using background music to affect the behavior of supermarket shoppers. *Journal of Marketing* 46, 86–91.

Muikku, J. (2001). *Musiikkia kaikkiruokaisille: Suomalaisen populaarimusiikin äänitetuotanto 1945–1990.* Helsinki: Gaudeamus.

Nettl, B. (2005 [1983]). *The study of ethnomusicology: Thirty-one issues and concepts.* Urbana: University of Illinois Press.

North, A., Hargreaves, D., & McKendrick, J. (1999). The influence of in-store music on wine selections. *Journal of Applied Psychology* 84(2), 271–6. https://doi.org/10.1037/0021-9010.84.2.271.

Nowak, R., & Bennett, A. (2014). Analysing everyday sound environments: The space, time and corporality of musical listening. *Cultural Sociology* 8(4), 426–42.

Nyman, J. (2005). *Suomi soi 4: Suuri suomalainen listakirja.* Helsinki: Tammi.

Partanen, E., Ahomäki, M., & Levola, M. (2020). *Musiikinkäyttötutkimus 2020*. Helsinki: Säveltäjäin Tekijänoikeustoimisto Teosto ry.

Payne, J., Korczynski, M., & Cluley, R. (2017). Hearing music in service interactions: A theoretical and empirical analysis. *Human Relations* 70(12), 1417–41. https://doi.org/10.1177/0018726717701552.

Pinch, T., & Bijsterveld, K. (2004). Sound studies: New technologies and music. *Social Studies of Science* 34(5), 635–48.

Radano, R. (1989). Interpreting Muzak: Speculations on musical experience in everyday life. *American Music* 7(4), 448–60. https://doi.org/10.2307/3051915.

Ramsey, S. (2022). *Car ownership report: Where in Europe is car ownership the highest and how much does this cost drivers?* www.confused.com/car-insurance/car-ownership-report (Accessed 20 Dec. 2022).

Ranta, A. (2005). Kulutuksen soivat kulissit. In O. Ampuja and K. Kilpiö, eds., *Kuultava menneisyys: suomalaista äänimaiseman historiaa*. Turku: UTUkirjat, pp. 257–78.

Rice, T. (2014). *Ethnomusicology: A very short introduction*. Oxford: Oxford University Press.

Riikonen, T. (1981). *Musiikista muzakiksi: Taustamusiikki teollistuneen joukkotiedotusyhteiskunnan työlauluna*. Master's thesis, University of Tampere.

Ringler, C., Esmark Jones, C. L., & Stevens, J. L. (2022). The ostrich effect: Feeling hidden amidst the ambient sound of human voices. *Journal of Retailing* 98(2), 593–610. https://doi.org/10.1016/j.jretai.2022.02.001.

Savage, M. (2021). Spotify wants to suggest song based on your emotions. *BBC Entertainment & Arts*. www.bbc.com/news/entertainment-arts-55839655 (Accessed 25 Jan. 2023).

Schafer, R. M. (1977). *The tuning of the world*. Toronto: McCelland and Stewart Limited.

Schmidt, U. (2023). *A philosophy of ambient sound: Materiality, technology, art and the sonic environment*. Singapore: Palgrave.

Sillanpää, M. (2002). *Säännöstelty huvi: Suomalainen ravintola 1900-luvulla*. Helsinki: Finnish Literature Society.

Small, C. (1998). *Musicking: The meanings of performing and listening*. Middletown, CT: Wesleyan University Press.

Smith, P. C., & Curnow, R. (1966). 'Arousal hypothesis' and the effects of music on purchasing behavior. *Journal of Applied Psychology* 50, 255–60.

Smolicki, J., ed. (2023). *Soundwalking: Through time, space, and technologies*. London: Routledge.

Spence, C., Puccinelli, N. M., Grewal, D., & Roggeveen, L. (2014). Store atmospherics: A multisensory perspective. *Psychology and Marketing* 31(7), 472–88.

Stenbäck, O. (2016). *Den ofrivilliga lyssnaren: Möten med butiksmusik*. Gothenburg Doctoral Dissertations, University of Gothenburg.

Sterne, J. (1997). Sounds like the Mall of America: Programmed music and the architectonics of commercial space. *Ethnomusicology* 41(1), 22–50. https:// doi.org/10.2307/852577.

Sterne, J. (2003). *The audible past: Cultural origins of sound reproduction.* Durham, NC: Duke University Press.

Sterne, J. (2013). The non-aggressive music deterrent. In M. G. Quiñones, A. Kassabian, & E. Boschi, eds., *Ubiquitous musics: The everyday sounds that we don't always notice.* Farnham: Ashgate, pp. 121–37.

Stockfelt, O. (1994). Cars, buildings and soundscapes. In H. Järviluoma, ed., *Soundscapes: Essays on Vroom and Moo.* Tampere: University of Tampere, pp. 19–38.

Stockfelt, O. (1997). Adequate modes of listening. In D. Schwarz D, A. Kassabian, & L. Siegel, eds., *Keeping score: Music, disciplinarity, culture.* Charlottesville, VA: University Press of Virginia.

Tagg, P. (1984). *Understanding musical time sense: Concepts, sketches and consequences.* www.tagg.org/articles/timesens.html (Accessed 14 Jan. 2022).

Teosto (2019). *Teosto. Avoimuusraportti.* Helsinki: Teosto.

Teosto (2022). *Teosto 90 vuotta*: https://historia.teosto.fi. (Accessed Jan 14, 2022).

Thibaud, J.-P. (2020). The hypothesis of ambient sensitivity. Invited lecture at Urban-Related Sensoria: Environments, Technologies, Sensobiographies, 12 June 2020, University of Eastern Finland.

Thompson, E. (2002). *The soundscape of modernity: Architectural acoustics and the culture of listening in America, 1900–1933.* Cambridge, MA: MIT Press.

Thrift, N. (2004). Intensities of feeling: Towards a spatial politics of affect. *Geografiska Annaler: Series B, Human Geography* 86(1), 57–78.

Tosoni, S., & Ridell, S. (2016). Decentering media studies, verbing the audience: Methodological considerations concerning people's uses of media in urban space. *International Journal of Communication* 10, 1277–93.

Trotta, F. (2020). *Annoying music in everyday life.* London: Bloomsbury.

Truax, B. (2001). *Acoustic communication.* 2nd ed. Westport, CT: Ablex.

Tynan, J., & Godson, L. (2019). *Uniform: Clothing and discipline in the modern world.* London: Bloomsbury. http://doi.org/10.5040/9781350045583.

Uimonen, H. (2005). *Ääntä kohti: Ääniympäristön kuuntelu, muutos ja merkitys.* Acta Universitatis Tamperensis 1110. Tampere: Tampere University Press.

Uimonen, H. (2011). *Radiomusiikin rakennemuutos: Kaupallisten radioiden musiikki 1985–2005.* Tampere: Tampere University Press.

Uimonen, H. (2014). Sulho Ranta ja radio. Musiikkiteknologian muutos tutkimuksen haasteena. In O. Heikkinen, K. Kilpiö, M. Mantere, et al., eds., *Valistus on viritetty: Esseitä musiikista, huvittelusta ja historiasta.* Sibelius-Akatemian julkaisuja 13, pp. 251–67.

Uimonen, H. (2017). Beyond the playlist: Commercial radio as music culture. *Popular Music* 36(2), 178–95. https://doi.org/10.1017/S0261143017000071.

Uimonen, H. (2020a). Käytännön kanonisointia: Radiomusiikin sisällöt ja muuttuva mediaympäristö. In S. Mononen, J. Palkisto, & I. Rantakallio, eds., *Musiikki ja merkityksenanto: Juhlakirja Susanna Välimäelle.* Helsinki: Suoni, pp. 255–77.

Uimonen, H. (2020b). Sensobiography and tangible music: Theoretical and methodological approaches. *Musiikki* 50(4), 42–68. https://musiikki.jour nal.fi/article/view/101313.

Uimonen, H. (2022a). Taustamusiikkipalvelut ja toimijuus: kulttuurinen lähestymistapa jokapaikkaisen musiikin valintaprosesseihin. *Musiikki* 54(1), 6–30. https://doi.org/10.51816/musiikki.115711.

Uimonen, H. (2022b). Radio Suomen ja Rádio Novan ohjelmasisällöt taustamusiikkiteollisuutena. *Media & viestintä* 45(1), 1–22.

Uimonen, H., & Kytö M. (2020). Toimimatonta tekniikkaa ja alitajuista vaikuttamista: Etnomusikologinen näkökulma taustamusiikin tutkimukseen. *Etnomusikologian vuosikirja 2020* 32, 46–75. https://doi.org/10.23985/ evk.90066.

Uimonen, H., Kytö, M., & Ruohonen, K. (2017). *Muuttuvat suomalaiset äänimaisemat.* Tampere: Tampere University Press. https://doi.org/ 10.26530/OAPEN_624254.

Uotinen, J. (2010). Kokemuksia autoetnografiasta. In J. Pöysä, H. Järviluoma, & S. Vakimo, eds., *Vaeltavat metodit.* Joensuu: SKTS, pp. 178–89.

Valkonen, T. (1985). Alueelliset erot. In T. Valkonen, R. Alapuro, M. Alestalo, R. Jallinoja, & T. Sandlund, eds., *Suomalaiset: Yhteiskunnan rakenne teollistumisen aikana.* Porvoo: WSOY, pp. 201–42.

Wiio, J. (2007). Suomalaisen television virstanpylväitä. In J. Wiio, ed., *Television viisi vuosikymmentä: Suomalainen televisio ja sen ohjelmat 1950-luvulta digiaikaan.* Helsinki: SKS, pp. 581–7.

Wiki (2023). Broadcast clock. *Wikipedia.* https://en.wikipedia.org/wiki/ Broadcast_clock.

Yeoh, J. P. S., & North, A. C. (2010). The effects of musical fit on choice between two competing foods. *Musicae Scientiae* 14(1), 165–80.

Zander, Mark F. (2006). Musical influences in advertising: How music modifies first impressions of product endorsers and brands. *Psychology of Music* 34(4), 465–80. https://doi.org/10.1177/0305735606067158.

Zuboff, S. (2015). Big other: Surveillance capitalism and the prospects of an information civilization. *Journal of Information Technology* 30, 75–89. https://doi.org/10.1057/jit.2015.5.

Cambridge Elements ≡

Music and the City

Simon Mcveigh
University of London
Simon Mcveigh is Professor of Music at Goldsmiths, University of London, and President of the Royal Musical Association. His research focuses on British musical life 1700–1945; and on violin music and performance practices of the period. Books include *Concert Life in London from Mozart to Haydn*(Cambridge) and *The Italian Solo Concerto 1700–1760* (Boydell).Current work centres on London concert life around 1900: a substantial article on the London Symphony Orchestra was published in 2013 and a book exploring London's musical life in the Edwardian era is in preparation for Boydell. He is also co-investigator on the digital concert-programme initiative *InConcert*.

Abigail Wood
University of Haifa
Abigail Wood is Senior Lecturer in Ethnomusicology at the Department of Music, School of Arts, University of Haifa, and past editor of Ethnomusicology Forum. Her research focuses primarily on musical life in contemporary urban spaces, from new musical spaces among religious Jewish women, to the reflection of the Israeli-Palestinian conflict in the contested soundscapes of Jerusalem's Old City.

About the Series
Elements in Music and the City sets urban musical cultures within new global and cross-disciplinary perspectives.
The series aims to open up new ways of thinking about music in an urban context, embracing the widest diversity of music and sound in cities across the world. Breaking down boundaries between historical and contemporary, and between popular and high art, it seeks to illuminate the diverse urban environment in all its exhilarating and vivid complexity. The urban thus becomes a microcosm of a much messier, yet ultimately much richer, conception of the 'music of everyday life'.
Rigorously peer-reviewed and written by leading scholars in their fields, each Element offers authoritative and challenging approaches towards a fast-developing area of music research. Elements in Music and the City will present extended case-studies within a comparative perspective, while developing pioneering new theoretical frameworks for an emerging field.
The series is inherently cross-disciplinary and global in its perspective, as reflected in the wide-ranging multinational advisory board. It will encourage a similar diversity of approaches, ranging from the historical and ethnomusicological to contemporary popular music and sound studies.
Written in a clear, engaging style without the need for specialist musical knowledge, *Elements in Music and the City* aims to fill the demand for easily accessible, quality texts available for teaching and research. It will be of interest not only to researchers and students in music and related arts but also to a broad range of readers intrigued by how we might understand music and sound in its social, cultural and political contexts.

Cambridge Elements $\overline{\overline{=}}$

Music and the City

Printed in the United States
by Baker & Taylor Publisher Services